ON A PERSONAL NOTE:

The Best Advice I Ever Got

The Best Advice I Ever Got

LESSONS *from* EXTRAORDINARY LIVES

KATIE COURIC

RANDOM HOUSE | NEW YORK

Published in the United States by Random House,
an imprint of The Random House Publishing Group,
a division of Random House, Inc., New York.

RANDOM HOUSE and colophon are
registered trademarks of Random House, Inc.

The source notes and permissions acknowledgments
begin on page 257.

LIBRARY OF CONGRESS CATALOGING-IN-PUBLICATION DATA
Couric, Katie.
The best advice I ever got : lessons from extraordinary lives /
by Katie Couric.
p. cm.
Includes bibliographical references.
ISBN 978-0-8129-9277-9
eBook ISBN 978-0-679-64386-9
1. Life skills. 2. Social skills. 3. Social ethics. 4. Lifestyles. I. Title.
HQ2037.C68 2011
646.7009'045—dc22   2010053892

Printed in the United States of America on acid-free paper

www.atrandom.com

2 4 6 8 9 7 5 3 1

FIRST EDITION

Book design by Casey Hampton

To my mom and dad, John and Elinor Couric,
for raising me with patience and humor
and my daughters, Ellie and Carrie Monahan,
for teaching me the importance of both

CONTENTS

CONTENTS

PART 2: THE BANK OF EXPERIENCE
On Hard Work and Tenacity

PART 3: NEVER GIVE IN
On Pluck and Perseverance

CONTENTS

PART 4: BE UNREASONABLE
On Passion and Dreams

CONTENTS

PART 7: EVERYONE NEEDS A CHEERLEADER
On Mentors and Encouragement

PART 8: LOOK OUTSIDE YOURSELF
On Commitment and Contribution

PART 9: WHAT BOATS ARE BUILT FOR
On Taking Risks and Seeking Opportunity

BORN ON A SUNNY DAY

M y husband, Jay, used to tell people that I was born on a sunny day. I thought it was the nicest compliment I ever received. I guess you could say I've always been one of those upbeat, glass-half-full people. Experts in the field of positive psychology might conclude that I'm "hardwired for happiness." When I was a little girl, the youngest of four, my sister Kiki's friends nicknamed me Smiley. Naturally outgoing and eager to please, I used to memorize photos in the yearbook and then approach various students at football games with salutations like "Hi! You're Barbara McLaughlin. I recognize you from the picture in my sister's yearbook!" Before you gag from the absolute adorableness of it all, to paraphrase that L'Oréal commercial, "Don't hate me because I'm happy." Trust me, I've been to the other side. My mom, a practitioner of common sense who was raised in Omaha, Nebraska, has often said that no one leaves this life unscathed. Indeed, dark clouds did come rolling in, and I've survived my share of window-rattling, life-shattering storms. But that comes later.

Growing up in Arlington, Virginia, I had a childhood that was more like *Leave It to Beaver* than *Modern Family*. Mine was an old-fashioned nuclear family, with a stay-at-home mom who, had she been born in a different time, would probably be an ad executive or a stockbroker (she bought many shares of Trojan condoms in the safe-sex early eighties), and a father who was thoughtful and intelligent, hardworking, a voracious reader, and a bit of a taskmaster who expected excellence from all four of his children. Add to that three older siblings, who paved the way for each one who followed, and a neighborhood teeming with kids who spent endless hours playing Red Light/Green Light and street baseball (with a tennis ball, since no gloves were used) and waging some pretty serious crab-apple fights, and you have an upbringing straight out of a Norman Rockwell painting.

Our recreational pursuits put many of the neighborhood kids on the injured reserve list. My own mishaps are, of course, the most vivid in my memory. Having just learned to ride bikes at age six, some of my neighborhood girlfriends and I decided to ride down the hilly sidewalk of Fortieth Street, single file, Indian style. It would have been an impressive showing of our newfound talents if only my best friend Sara Crosman had also learned to use the brakes. Instead, at the bottom of the hill her bike crashed into mine (I was leading the pack, I'm slightly embarrassed to admit) and threw me forward. My chin came down on the sidewalk, and the impact broke one of my proudest possessions: my new front tooth. My mom cried, her tears, I'm still convinced, more for financial than cosmetic concerns, and I spent many of my elementary school years sporting a silver tooth in class photos—a lovely addition to my horrifying inch-long bangs. When Chris Foley tripped me on the blacktop after I stuck my tongue out at him in third grade, it was a bit of a godsend. Two caps looked less fake than one.

So the memories of my youth are a collection of happy snapshots: cheerleading, running track, playing the piano, piling into our station wagon for an occasional vacation to the beach as we demolished the sandwiches my mom had made for lunch by 9 A.M., taking my sister Emily to New York to travel across the ocean to spend her junior year abroad while she was at Smith College, going to my brother Johnny's baseball and basketball games, watching my sister Kiki driving off in my dad's racing-green Sunbeam Alpine (his one midlife indulgence), her pom-poms peeking out as she headed to a high school football game.

The accompanying score would be provided by ten years of Debussy and Chopin, courtesy of my piano teacher, Mrs. Richmond. I was the only one in my family who kept up with lessons, but because I play by ear, and, like Irving Berlin, play everything in the key of C, I often slacked off when it came to actually reading music. But I still love to sit down, even today, and figure out a song I've just heard or dust off some classical pieces from my early years. All these things made up a childhood that gave me a healthy sense of who I was and no boundaries for what I might become, although at the time I had no idea. To some, it might seem pretty ordinary. For me, it was heaven.

I often wish that I could bottle my parents' special recipe for raising happy, healthy, successful children. My dad always encouraged us to do our best, and there was accountability when we didn't. A cerebral, gentle man, but a tough disciplinarian, when he called to us and we responded, "Yes," he would say, "Yes what?" We were required to answer, "Yes, sir," although my brother Johnny, who had a slight lisp when he was little, would say, "Yeth, thir!" My mom, funny and creative, was the personification of the adage "An idle mind is the devil's playground." Saying "I'm bored" was tantamount to committing murder, and we were always enrolled in summer school, primarily because she wanted us out of her hair. One summer, when all the other classes were full, she put Emily, a stellar student, in remedial reading, which clearly helped her graduate Phi Beta Kappa from Smith College.

My mom's motto was "Let 'em know you're there!" She obviously wasn't keen on raising vanilla shrinking violets. But both my parents gave each of us the launching pad we needed to succeed, and my siblings and I felt their presence in everything we did. The best illustration may be the joint-task-force nature of school elections. My dad would help us write our speeches, like the one in which my sister Kiki promised to break all records as recording secretary and then promptly broke one of my dad's old LPs on her knee with dramatic flair. My fifth-grade vice-presidential speech adopted the Underdog strategy (the cartoon, that is), as I told my elementary school, "Never fear, Katie's here." Meanwhile, my mom, the artistic one, was in charge of making posters. She cut up fake money into letters when my brother Johnny ran for student-council treasurer. She also came up with catchy slogans for my sister's campaigns, like the one on a poster that was placed above the water fountain at school, boasting FREE WATER, COURTESY EMILY COURIC FOR PRESIDENT! Growing up in our house was a fun-filled family affair, and it got a little bit lonelier every time one of my older siblings headed off to college.

I fully anticipated the same kind of family setting when I became an adult, and at first it looked as though I might have it. I married a man who was fun-loving, brilliant, and oozing with integrity. (And he could dance! And I love to dance!) We had two healthy little girls, a marriage that had highs and lows but a rock-solid foundation, and our careers were going swimmingly. When we married, Jay was an associate at a prestigious Washington law firm, Williams & Connolly, and I had just been hired to cover the Pentagon. After we wed, his closest friend and fellow lawyer, David Kiernan, changed the name that appeared on his phone when he was making outgoing calls from Jay Monahan to Jay Couric. A traditional guy who was also proud of my accomplishments, Jay found it mildly amusing.

I remember bringing our second daughter, Carrie, home from the hospital in January 1996 following—use overly dramatic weatherman voice here—"the blizzard of the century!" and settling into our warm apartment. She was napping with me and Ellie, then four and a half, while Jay played a Brahms lullaby on the Steinway piano that we had bought each other for our birthdays, which were two days apart. This was deeper and more satisfying than any happiness I'd ever experienced. This was pure, soul-filling contentment.

That was BC. Before cancer. That jarring transition was exactly how it felt. Just fifteen months after Carrie was born, Jay was diagnosed with stage-four colon cancer and we were pulled into a swirling vortex of panic, depression, anxiety, and fear. We were desperate to find any reason to hope, but the situation, I can only now admit, was hopeless. When I told my mother-in-law, Carol (who was herself undergoing treatment for ovarian cancer), that the doctor had informed me that there were tumors all over Jay's liver, she responded with a deflated and uncharacteristic "Shit." What followed were nine months of brutal treatments, endless futile searches for newly discovered therapies, and copious quantities of denial. We never talked about the fact that Jay might die. Acknowledging that made it too real. The closest thing to a discussion of the possibility of death came when I told Jay that if something happened to him, I didn't think I could come to the country house we had just bought. I couldn't imagine going there, to his dream house, without him. "Well," he said, cushioning the blow of his almost guaranteed absence, "I hope it will be full of happy memories." He died after collapsing on the floor of our powder room on January 24, 1998. The life I had imagined and cherished was also buried on a freezing, windy January afternoon.

When my sister Emily was diagnosed with pancreatic cancer just two years later, it seemed too much to bear. She was a rising political star in Virginia and many expected her to be the first female governor of the state. But to me she was my smart, beautiful, and driven oldest sister who set a high bar for all the Couric kids. Just as Jay had, she fought like hell, with grace and guts. She was also a wonderful wife and the mother of two fantastic sons. My first four decades of life seemed to be getting some kind of psychic payback. Two of the finest people I've ever known were infuriatingly ripped off, as were all the people who loved them.

When Jay was in the midst of his battle with cancer, I resented people laughing over lunch at a crowded café, walking their babies in strollers, the women whose biggest problems involved which sweater they were going to buy that day. I wanted to shake my fists at them and yell, "How can you be enjoying yourselves? My whole world is falling apart!" I now realize that everyone struggles, and that my mom was right: Very few of us get through this life unscathed. Scratch beneath a stranger's surface and you're likely to uncover professional setbacks, broken hearts, unspeakable loss, unfulfilled dreams, or worse. Everyone seems to keep going but, God knows, navigating through it all isn't easy.

How do you keep going when you want to curl up into a ball and never leave your bedroom? How do you squeeze all the joy out of life while dealing with all the messy parts? How can you find a calling that fills you up, gives you a sense of purpose and your life meaning, and doesn't leave you feeling full of regret and remorse? How do you shut out the voices (including, at times, your own) that tell you you're not good enough and you shouldn't even try? How can you "recalculate" your route when your personal GPS is on the fritz?

These are questions we all ask ourselves at one time or another. I know I have. But I've always found comfort and guidance in hearing from people who have wrestled with the same questions and, through the simple act of living, have found their own versions of the right answers.

Their stories are sometimes found in books, like Katharine Graham's *Personal History,* or in speeches, like Theodore Roosevelt's "Man in the Arena." But I've also found inspiration in an unlikely place: the commencement address. I've given a dozen through the years, and I'm always interested in what other speakers have to say. These addresses are often thoughtful, entertaining, and very personal. And, like eulogies celebrating a life well lived, they make you want to be a better version of yourself.

Last year, when I was giving the commencement address at Case Western Reserve University in Cleveland, I decided to try something new. What else could I tell these young, bright students who were about to take flight into the world, eager to make their mark? Because I've had the privilege of meeting and interviewing so many remarkable people through the years, I decided to ask a few of them to share their personal insights. What have you learned? What lessons from your own lives might be useful and instructive? I reached out to about thirty people, and after a few weeks many of them reached back to me with their responses. I couldn't wait to open their emails, which were moving and funny and profound and helpful—even for someone my age. They made me realize that this advice should be shared, not simply with college graduates but with anyone who may be in need of a little lift, a little instruction . . . or a few laughs. So I cast an even wider net, hoping to convince leaders and visionaries in the fields of politics, entertainment, sports, philanthropy, the arts, and business to participate. Again, I was amazed by the response and the generosity of so many people, even those I'd never met. Some people fired back their advice and anecdotes in record speed; others took their time, and seemed to agonize over the responsibility of passing on life lessons in just the right way; some folks allowed us to adapt their own commencement speeches, many of which I had heard about through the grapevine from friends whose children attended those schools, and some of these contributors had never allowed their speeches to be printed elsewhere before this book; some people adapted reflections and episodes from their own books and writings (hey, if it ain't broke, don't fix it). Uniformly, though, the response was a verbal high-five, as if to say "Hey, I've been there, too." Each story collected in this book was thoughtfully submitted and lovingly, often painstakingly, crafted. I was further struck by how inspired I was by these words, despite the fact that I am fifty-four years old and well into my career. They aren't just for those who are starting out; they're for those who are starting over, or just taking stock—a reminder of what is important and how we can better live our lives every day.

I found that people were especially happy to share their stories for a worthy cause. I have partnered with Scholarship America, a nonprofit scholarship and educational support organization founded in 1958 that has made it possible for students across the country to achieve their college dreams. I've heard and read many stories of Scholarship America students whose lives were forever changed by the gift of education beyond high school. Students like Matt, a high achiever with a twin brother and a younger sister whose middle-class family couldn't afford to send him to his dream school until Scholarship America's Dollars for Scholars program made it possible. Or Molly, whose plans for a nursing career were put on hold when her husband's trucking business went belly-up due to soaring gasoline prices, until Scholarship America's Dreamkeepers program allowed her to stay in school and get her degree. Nothing is more gratifying than hearing stories of those who "pay it forward"—people like Rain, a young woman who immigrated to the United States from China at age six and used her scholarship to pursue a career at a nonprofit that provides services to New York City children; or Linda, the daughter of a single Mexican-American mother of six, who won a scholarship and is now attending UCLA with the hopes of becoming a doctor. And then there's Jay, now in his sixties, who received a $300 scholarship back in 1969 when public school tuition was $200. Jay was able to earn his MBA, go on to a successful career in finance, and then, in his retirement years, volunteer for a local chapter of Scholarship America—talk about coming full circle.

Scholarship America's programs have had a huge financial impact on the lives of students across the country, but as I've learned, it's about more than just dollars and cents. It's also about giving students confidence, inspiration, and some supportive words to carry with them: "I believe in you." That's what a scholarship really says. And that's why it seems only fitting to me that all of my proceeds from this book—a collection of lessons learned from extraordinary lives—will provide scholarships to help others realize their full potential so that their own stories and advice may one day appear in a book like this.

So I'd like to thank all the people who have had an impact on my life, and all those here who have given us permission to present their stories of winning and losing, setbacks and callbacks, ups and downs. Oscar Wilde once said, "I always pass on good advice. It is the only thing to do with it. It is never of any use to oneself." I hope you'll find these words as compelling, fun to read—and, yes, wise—as I have. And, wherever you are in your journey, I hope you'll feel inspired to share your own.

PART 1

YOU'VE GOTTA HAVE MOXIE

On Courage and Self-Confidence

Courage is being scared to death but saddling up anyway.

— JOHN WAYNE

My dad encouraged me to go into journalism. He had worked as a reporter for the *Macon Telegraph, The Atlanta Constitution,* and United Press before going into public relations to earn a salary that could better support four kids. During the summers that I was a student at the University of Virginia, he encouraged me to work at radio stations in Washington, D.C. This was long before internship programs for college students were commonplace, so I got out the yellow pages and started calling radio stations and asking if I could come in and apply for a summer job. I ended up working at three different radio stations by the time I had graduated, and decided that TV might be an even more exciting, not to mention lucrative, career choice. I loved to write and could do it quickly, thanks to years of procrastinating (I still remember my dad's bemusement as his fifth-grade daughter sat cross-legged just inside the front door, frantically finishing her homework before running for the bus), and I loved people. I was, yes, perky, damn it—a description of me that I came to abhor—and, perhaps more important, insatiably curious. And, let's face it, I had plenty of drive and ambition, the kind that started slowly simmering after college and came to a full, rolling boil when I found myself in a competitive work environment. But after graduating from college with a BA in American studies I realized that landing a job in TV news was going to be a challenge. I had sent out résumés and made calls, but getting my proverbial foot in the door just wasn't happening. So one morning I put on my best "dress for success" outfit—you know, the blue blazer, the blouse, the completely geeky little bow tied around my collar, which was the almost obligatory wardrobe for any young, aspiring career woman at the time. I got into our family's cream-colored Buick station wagon and asked my mom to drive me to the ABC News bureau in Washington, D.C.

Even though I had sent in a résumé months earlier, every time I called the deputy bureau chief, Kevin Delaney, to ask if I could come in for an interview, his officious secretary blew me off. I thought I'd just go down there to see if I could be more convincing in person. I got out of the car, walked into the ABC News building, and asked the physically imposing security guard if I could see Kevin Delaney. When he discovered that I was a walk-in, the guard chuckled and said that I couldn't see Mr. Delaney without an appointment. Undeterred, I asked if I could use the phone in the waiting area, dialed the operator, and said in a determined voice, "Can you connect me to Davey Newman, the executive producer of *World News Tonight*?" Luckily, he answered his own phone. "Hi, Davey," I blurted out. "You don't know me, but your twin brothers, Steve and Eddie, went to high school with my sister Kiki, and I live down the street from your cousin Julie." He listened patiently as I rambled on. After convincing him of our close, almost familial connections, I asked if I could come up to the newsroom and poke my head into the deputy bureau chief's office. I think he was completely flummoxed by our phone conversation and said, "Sure, come on up." He dutifully dropped me off at Kevin Delaney's door, and the secretary who wouldn't give me the time of day watched powerlessly as I waltzed in.

I chatted with Mr. Delaney and told him that I really wanted to work at ABC News. I told him I had a considerable amount of work experience compared with many of my peers and would be a real asset to the organization. I let him know that I was there, and then some! But he was most impressed by my ability to worm my way into his office and seemed amused when I briefed him on "Operation Delaney." He actually moved my résumé from near the bottom of the pile to the top. I was hired a few weeks later.

Where I got the nerve, at twenty-two, to do this, I'm still not sure. Maybe I have my mom to thank. I got my first job in TV news and made incredible contacts. My first day at work, the colorful ABC White House correspondent Sam Donaldson jumped on a desk, sang "K-K-K-Katie" at the top of his lungs, and swept me away to a White House news conference. That day it was my turn to be flummoxed.

When it comes to going for a job, a promotion, or just about anything in life, I'm pretty convinced that the meek will not inherit the earth. You've got to find a way to make yourself stand out from the pack, whether it's burning your résumé onto a baseball bat, as a friend of mine did when she was applying for a job with the Florida Marlins, carrying around business cards *before* you're hired—cards you can give to someone you've met at a party or on the train—or finding your own trademark, as Mario Batali has with his orange clogs. Whether you call it chutzpah, cojones (as former Secretary of State Madeleine Albright has said), or one of my dad's favorite words, moxie, it's an essential ingredient for success—unless you're so talented that people are knocking down your door and you don't have to try to get into theirs. And if that's the case, I hate you.

Mario Batali
Celebrity Chef and Restaurateur

Life Is Not a Recipe

My first job objective after college was to hold on to the job I had while I was in college. It was at Stuff Yer Face, a landmark stromboli and beer joint on Easton Avenue on the Rutgers University main campus. It was my first restaurant job, and I liked it. I started out washing dishes and eventually became the fastest line cook in the place. On second thought, Mitchell Ostrander was faster. But I had more flair.

Anyway, what I got out of that first job—besides a serious addiction to the adrenaline rush of working at full tilt in a restaurant kitchen that I never recovered from—was a sense of confidence about who I was. I learned that I liked working extremely hard. I learned that I could handle stress by kidding around and keeping it real. And I learned what may just have been the most useful piece of knowledge of my entire career to date: how to clean a blisteringly hot deep-fat fryer filled with stinking grease and detritus—and why you have to do it, disgusting as it may be.

I'm not kidding. It turns out to be a metaphor. Cleanliness is next to tastiness. Cook with a dirty fryer and you cook garbage. Start with a clean fryer and you get something perfect, simple, and poetic. Just like all of cooking, and all of life. Garbage in, garbage out. Truth in, truth out.

One day, not long after I graduated from college, I woke up and realized that I'd learned all I was going to learn from cleaning that deep fryer at Stuff Yer Face—and that I was hooked on the idea of the restaurant business, even if I wasn't sure exactly what that meant. So I took off for London and signed up for cooking classes at the Cordon Bleu. Whatever. I got a job working at a pub, where the chef was this crazed Brit named Marco. At the time, he was just a cook with a nasty temper who threw things at people—a working-class half-Italian kid from the slums of Leeds. But I could tell there was some kind of weird but formidable genius there. So I stuck it out and learned what I could from his inventive, balls-of-steel cooking style.

We were both in our early twenties. In the next few years, he morphed into Marco Pierre White, one of the most famous, flashiest, and wealthiest chefs in the world. He's a brilliant, media-savvy entrepreneur, and he's always known how to make himself larger than life. I hated the guy, but I have to say, rubbing shoulders with him just when I did taught me how to think on a much larger scale and got me interested in becoming a chef with a real, bold point of view. Working under him also taught me the value of not being an asshole, and I'm actually still grateful for that. But, most of all, what I got out of that experience was: You gotta get a brand.

Stuff Yer Face and Greasy Tony's were my two hangouts when I was at Rutgers, and looking back, I realize they were the first places I ever had brand loyalty to. I would walk half a mile at night all the way from the River dorms—Campbell 614—just to spend four bucks on a boli or a cheese steak. You see, the thing I knew back then, just as now, is that brand loyalty is all about truth and heart.

I buy a lot of stuff, usually on the Internet. I buy what I feel like buying, and I don't think much about who I'm buying it from. I fly on whatever airline is going where I want to go. Who cares? But when it comes to restaurants, that's where I feel brand loyalty. There are restaurants all over the world that have me exactly where the marketing people at Coors or Nike or Lexus would love to have me. And that's because those restaurants have carved out a little corner of my heart and my mind and planted something true, real, consistent, and creative that makes me want to come back.

That's what Marco Pierre White figured out. And that's what I learned along the way, too. For better or for worse, I've got a brand. The orange clogs, the ponytail, the attitude, my seeming fluency in Italian. It's instantly recognizable. But what matters to me is it's not fake.

What I started figuring out after I left school and began poking around the world is that you've got to pay attention to the truth. It's not an intellectual thing—it's a gut thing. My truth is that I love real, honest, passionate, intense experiences. Experiences that don't apologize for themselves or claim to be something they aren't. That's what I want to give people when they eat in my restaurants or watch my shows or read my books. Truth, passion, intense hits of joy. That's my brand. Trust me. It sounds cheesy, but it's not. Sooner or later, you've got to get a brand. And I'm not talking about marketing or focus groups or giving a second thought to what anyone else thinks. The kind of brand I'm talking about is nothing more—and nothing less—than your own truth, expressed consistently by you.

I'm Italian. It's a huge part of who I am. I grew up in a big family of brilliant home cooks who had that Italian killer instinct about food and celebration and connecting with people. And I spent a lot of time in Italy growing up. So after cooking in London and San Francisco and Santa Barbara, in places like the Four Seasons Hotel, I figured something out. Just as college-level econ courses can prepare you only so much for the real world, cooking schools and hotel kitchens can teach you only so much about cooking. The rest you've got to find and experience for yourself. And, of course, there's no right answer. It's about finding what's true for you, and you know it when you see it. Me, I had a hunch that Italy was where I ought to look.

I asked my dad to write to some of his buddies in the restaurant business in Italy to ask if they knew about apprenticeships, jobs, dishwashing opportunities, whatever, and he sent out a bunch of letters. He got one response. It was from a tiny family-run trattoria in a town way up in the hills between Bologna and nowhere. That was all I needed to know.

I showed up a few weeks later with a small duffel bag and a guitar. The town, Borgo Capanne, is not much more than a few crappy little houses on either side of a windy mountain road. But there it was. Trattoria La Volta. Twenty-five seats. Fine crystal stemware. Exquisite table linens and silverware. And the kind of country elegance that is (a) quintessentially and uniquely Italian, (b) totally unpretentious, and (c) perfect. I had agreed to work there for a few months. I wound up staying for three years.

For me, La Volta was the ultimate cooking school and the ultimate window on the world. I'd been a sous-chef. I thought I knew how to cook. But Betta and Mara—the two women who ran the kitchen at La Volta—they were cooks. They knew truths they didn't even know they knew. And, as I worked and goofed around and hung out with them over those years, I didn't so much learn as internalize those truths.

I hardly even want to tell you what kind of truths they were. They sound like clichés. Things like the best food is the truly simple stuff of home cooks, made with perfect ingredients that reflect that place and that one moment in time. Or great Italian food comes not from opulence and extravagance but from poverty, invention, and honesty. I could go on all day. But what I'm really saying is that spending three years in the hills of Emilia-Romagna at that point in my life was the experience that made everything gel for me.

I hung out. I watched. I made an ass of myself. I became the only man in Emilia-Romagna to learn how to roll pasta by hand in a hundred years. But ultimately I made that experience my own. At some point, what you've taken in turns into your take on things, and comes back out as something original. I kind of knew it was happening and I kind of didn't. But the Mario I am today is the Mario I figured out I was at La Volta.

I came back to the U.S. and opened a restaurant in New York, where I took the ideas behind what I'd learned at Trattoria La Volta and reinvented them. I wanted people to feel like they were eating food that the kind of great Italian cooks at La Volta would make if they moved to New York and had really good local ingredients to work with. That's all. Just that simple idea. Well, it worked. And it still appears to be working.

The more fake and commercialized the world gets, the more people respond to things that have a real core of truth. I believe that every human being is hardwired to recognize that. Whatever you choose to do with your life—whether it's running a company or cooking dinner—

stand for something you know is true. If there's a recipe for success, it's staying real and true.

Which reminds me: Life is not a recipe. Recipes are just descriptions of one person's take on one moment in time. They're not rules. People think they are. They look as if they are. They say, "Do this, not this. Add this, not that." But, really, recipes are just suggestions that got written down.

You want a recipe? Boil some spaghetti in well-salted water. While you're doing that, heat up some good extra-virgin olive oil in a skillet and throw in thin slices of garlic and some red-pepper flakes. When the pasta's cooked, toss it in the skillet. Throw in some chopped parsley and a little of the pasta water. Toss it around. Put it on a plate. Grate some Parmigiano-Reggiano on top. Congratulations, dude. You've just made *spaghetti all'aglio e olio*. One of the greatest simple truths of humankind—and a damn good emergency dinner. That's a recipe. It's an idea. It's a dish. It's an icon. It's an experience. It's not rules. As you cook up your own life, never let anyone else's recipe for success intimidate you or get in your way. Know your own truth, and live by it.

Gail Collins

New York Times Op-Ed Columnist

————

Ask, and Ye Shall Receive

My story goes back to when I was in college, so we're talking about when dinosaurs roamed the earth. I wanted to be the editor of my school magazine. Actually, there were two co-editors, and tradition required that there be one male and one female. And they were selected by the faculty. (I told you it was a long time ago.)

A guy in my journalism class—let's call him Fred—came to me and said, "I have a proposal. Let's apply as a team. I know I'm conservative and you're liberal, but I'm interested in graphic arts and, honestly, I don't care what kind of Communist propaganda you put on the pages as long as I can make it look good."

Fred was worried about competition from another student we will call George. Obviously, George wasn't my problem, since I was going for the girl slot. But I did like the idea of being totally in charge of the words, so I signed on to Fred's plan.

The day of the faculty interviews arrived. Our rival, George, went first, then Fred. On his way out the door, George said to me, "I should tell you that I told them I only wanted to do this if I could work with you."

Fred was obviously not the only plotter on campus.

I had not had a chance to digest this information when I was called in for my interview. The dean said, "We have an interesting situation here, Gail. Our top two male candidates both want to work with you. So we've decided to let you choose your co-editor."

I stared at the assembled faculty members for a minute, and then I said, "Actually, I'd rather do it by myself."

————

The dean shrugged and said, "Okay."

I walked back to the dorm stunned at my gall, my treachery, and my totally unexpected triumph.

So the moral, and my best advice, is that you should always let people know what you want. Without being irritating, of course. Incessant nagging works well only if you're trying to get the landlord to fix a leak.

When I became an editor in the real world, I discovered that many people wait for their boss to decide what they should do next. Even if they're unhappy, they seem to feel that their boss knows better than they do what will make them feel more fulfilled.

This is generally a terrible approach. Having been an authority figure, I can tell you—we don't usually let this out, but I know I'm among friends—that your boss has no idea what is the best thing for you. Your boss is probably not a genius. Your boss is probably just like me, and has no objection whatsoever to making you happy, if there's a way to do it that doesn't make him or her unhappy in the process.

So figure out what you want. And then ask for it. The worst that can happen is that you'll wind up letting Fred do the graphics.

By the way, George and Fred both signed on as my assistant editors and we all got along great. Except for the fact that the quarterly magazine came out only three times that year. Which was totally my fault, really.

Bill Cosby
Emmy and Grammy Award–Winning Comedian, Actor,
Producer, and Bestselling Author

———

Don't Be Your Own Worst Enemy

In the late sixties, I was performing at a club in Chicago called the Gate of Horn. Even though it was a folk room, it was a nice, hip place and I was proud to work there. But across the street was a *really* big-time club.

Mr. Kelly's.

You see, in those days there were a whole bunch of clubs across the country—like Basin Street East in New York City, or the hungry i in San Francisco—that were *the* spots. They were on the same level as Mr. Kelly's. And the guys who played at these clubs—guys like Lenny Bruce, Dick Gregory, and Jonathan Winters—were making huge money: $2,500 a week! I was making $125. They were on *Ed Sullivan*; I had never been on TV.

The point is, these clubs were the pinnacle. The top. Once you played there, you were *big*-time. I often stared across the street and wondered, *Gee whiz, man, will I ever get to play Mr. Kelly's?* Then one day, when I was back in New York, I got the call. *The* call. From my agent. He told me he had gotten an offer for me to play Mr. Kelly's. Opening act at $350 a week—I had never made that much money in my life!

The brothers George and Oscar Marienthal owned Mr. Kelly's. I'm not sure if they were twins, but they looked a lot alike. Anyway, they had seen me somewhere—I don't know where—and obviously liked me, because they booked me. They flew me to Chicago, and I got a suite at the Hotel Maryland for twelve dollars a day, and then I went to Mr. Kelly's and put my clothes in the dressing room.

So, I was sitting in my dressing room in Mr. Kelly's, a small dressing room, and it was somewhere around two o'clock, and my mind started to tell me that I wasn't really funny enough to be in a club like Mr. Kelly's.

Flash! *You are not funny.*

The feeling would go away—I would *make* it go away—but from two o'clock until the first show at eight, I began, without moving my lips, to talk myself into the fact that I was not funny and that I really and truly had no business playing Mr. Kelly's:

These performers—they are on TV. They have proven themselves. And you? You're just a Temple University student, and I don't know what you think you're doing, but you certainly have no *business in front of this crowd, which is a hard-liquor crowd. These people have seen the best, and they're not going to see the best tonight.*

And so I beat myself down to a point of not believing that I was funny. I just knew that I wasn't going to do well.

But I went downstairs anyway.

I had a sport coat on, slacks, a tie. I looked good. I looked like a professional comedian. And then the fellow introduced me: "Ladies and gentlemen, Mr. Kelly's is proud to present one of the fastest-rising new comedians, Mr. Bill Cosby!"

And there I was. Onstage.

At Mr. Kelly's.

I forget who the headliner was, but the house was about half full. There were a hundred people there, and maybe sixty applauded. I did my act, which was supposed to last twenty-five minutes, in twelve minutes. Twenty-five minutes of comedy in twelve minutes.

There was no laughter.

Of course, I left no *time* for laughter. And certainly, while I was talking, those poor people in the audience didn't hear anything funny. I delivered my routine like a *speech,* and I did it in twelve minutes. And then I said, "Thank you very much and good night."

I waved at them, and the same people who had clapped me onto the stage did not clap me off.

I went up to the dressing room, and I had this horrible feeling that this was *it*—the end of my career. And I talked to myself again without moving my lips, and I tried to make myself feel better:

Okay, you've had a good time, but you certainly are not funny and you don't want to do this again. You don't ever want to do this again, because it's a horrible, horrible feeling.

So I was sitting in the dressing room and there was a knock on the door. It was George Marienthal. George came in and closed the door. I had both arms across my chest and I was bent over, and I never looked up. "Mr. Marienthal," I said, "I am very, very sorry for what happened, and I am very sorry for what I did tonight. I refuse to accept any pay from you."

"Good," Mr. Marienthal said. "'Cause you stink!"

"And as soon as I get the money I will pay you back for the plane trip, the hotel room, and everything else, but I will not be going out to do the second show. I am going back to Temple University."

"I think you should."

"I am going to play football and I am going to graduate from college and get my master's and my doctorate."

"Exactly!"

"So thank you very, very much for this opportunity, Mr. Marienthal. And I really apologize to you, but I will *not* be going back out on that stage."

"Good," Mr. Marienthal said. "You are not going back out on that stage because you, sir, are not good."

I felt terrible. Just terrible. But Mr. Marienthal didn't let up.

"You, sir, embarrassed me," he continued. "You embarrassed my brother. And, even though you embarrassed us, let me say that you don't have to pay us back one iota. You owe us nothing, sir. Just take your things with you and you may leave."

Mr. Marienthal started for the door, but stopped and turned around to face me. "Will you do me a favor?" he asked.

"Sure," I said. I would have done anything to feel less terrible, to somehow make amends.

"When you get back to your hotel," Mr. Marienthal said, "will you tell Bill Cosby to come back here and do the second show and to never again send you, because, sir, you are *not* funny. Bill Cosby is very, very funny. I don't know why he sent you. Probably because he was afraid.

Who knows what happens in the minds of entertainers? But, sir, *you* get out of here and you bring Bill Cosby—you *send* Bill Cosby. Do whatever, but Bill Cosby *has* to come back here and do the second show."

Mr. Marienthal opened the door, gave me a look, and said with emphasis, "Now, *you* get out. And don't forget, I want Bill Cosby back here."

I went back to the hotel. Despite what Mr. Marienthal had tried to do, it didn't lift my spirits. I didn't feel any better. I sat in the room wondering what I was going to do. Eventually, I went back to the club.

I was embarrassed and walked straight through the club with no sense of pride. Nobody said anything to me. A trio was playing some hip kind of jazz music, and the place seemed to have a few more people than the first show. I went up to the dressing room and I just sat there. Nobody came in. The flowers that had come with a note from the Marienthals welcoming me to Mr. Kelly's were still there—they hadn't taken them away. So I just sat there.

Showtime!

I went downstairs and I stood there. Two minutes to eleven. The trio stopped and the audience politely applauded, and I stood in the dark, ready to go on for this horrible, horrible punishment. There I was, standing in front of these people who had seen the best and the greatest, and now they were going to see the worst.

Eleven o'clock.

The announcer said, "Ladies and gentlemen . . . Bill Cosby."

Just that. Bill Cosby. No "fastest-rising." Nothing. And that introduction took me out of whatever self-pity I was wallowing in, because it hurt.

Ladies and gentlemen . . . Bill Cosby.

Bill Cosby? I knew I was better than that. *Whaddayamean, Bill Cosby? What happened?*

And I shouted as I walked onto the stage: "What happened to the part—you just said Bill Cosby—what happened to the part . . ."

The people began to chuckle, because they thought it was part of the routine. I said, "What? When you introduced me in the first show, you said I was one of the fastest-rising young, fastest-rising new comics. And now this time you just say Bill Cosby?"

The announcer—I don't remember who the fellow was—said, "That's because I saw the first show."

And the place broke up.

Now, ordinarily I guess this would have meant destruction for a performer. But for me, well, it just took me out of all that self-degradation. And I began to talk to the guy.

"Well," I said, "I'll tell you something, it *was* a terrible show."

And then Bill Cosby—the Bill Cosby in me—came out and I did about ten minutes on my behavior and the disastrous twelve-minute show. I didn't say anything about Mr. Marienthal, but I glanced toward the back. I hoped he was watching.

So I did twenty-five minutes, and I think only about seven minutes of prepared, written material. The applause was wonderful. I left the stage and headed up to my dressing room. I just sat there with my arms folded across my chest, rather relieved, but not completely. I still had some feelings of self-doubt:

Okay, okay. But there's tomorrow. Do I have to wait until eleven o'clock, when they're drunk?

There was a knock on the door. It was Mr. Marienthal. George. And he came into the dressing room.

"Bill, wonderful show," he said. "Who was that horrible fellow you sent for the first show?"

I looked up at him and I said, "Mr. Marienthal, I hope never to send him out on the stage again."

And Mr. Marienthal said, "If you do, you ought to really, before you even think about it, realize that there are some people out there who want to laugh."

Anna Quindlen

Bestselling Author and Pulitzer Prize–Winning Journalist

———

Courage Is the Ultimate Career Move

Here is my favorite biblical direction: Be not afraid. It's truly the secret of life. Fear is what stunts our growth, narrows our ambitions, kills our dreams.

So fear not.

Oh, I have enough of a memory of my own youth to know that that sounds preposterous. You are surely afraid: of leaving what you know, of seeking what you want, of taking the wrong path, of failing the right one. But you can't allow any of that to warp your life. You must have the strength to say no to the wrong things and to embrace the right ones, even if you are the only one who seems to know the difference, even if you find the difference hard to calculate.

Too often we still live with the pinched expectations of a culture of conformity, which sees daring as dangerous. Go along to get along: that's its mantra. Only a principled refusal to be terrorized by these stingy standards will save you from a Frankenstein life made up of other people's expectations grafted together into a poor imitation of existence. You can't afford to do that. It is what has poisoned our culture, our community, and our national character. No one does the right thing from fear, and so many of the wrong things are done in its long shadow. Homophobia, racism, religious bigotry: they are all bricks in a wall that divides us, bricks cast of the clay of fear, fear of that which is different or unknown.

Too often our public discourse fears real engagement or discussion; it pitches itself at the lowest possible level, always preaching to the choir, so that no one will be challenged. Which usually means that no one will be

———

interested. What is the point of free speech if we are always afraid to speak freely? If we fear competing viewpoints, if we fail to state the unpopular because of some sense of plain-vanilla civility, it is not civility at all. It is the denigration of the human capacity for thought. Open your mouth. Speak your piece. Fear not.

Remember Pinocchio? There is a Jiminy Cricket on your shoulder, giving the very best advice. It is you, your authentic self, the one you were in first grade, before you learned to massage your personality into a form that would suit others. Sometimes it's hard to hear its message because all the external voices are so loud, so shrill, so adamant. Voices that loud are always meant to bully.

Do not be bullied.

Acts of bravery don't always take place on battlefields. They can take place in your heart, when you have the courage to honor your character, your intellect, your inclinations, and, yes, your soul by listening to its clean, clear voice of direction instead of following the muddied messages of a timid world. So carry your courage in an easily accessible place, the way you do your cellphone or your wallet. You may still falter or fail, but you will always know that you pushed hard and aimed high. Take a leap of faith. Fear not. Courage is the ultimate career move.

Helen Mirren

Academy Award and Emmy-Winning Actress

Beware of Fear

My secondary school was a parochial school run by Bernardine nuns in forbidding black robes. On my first visit to the school, I had an interview with the headmistress. She was a very old lady called Dame Mother Mary Mildred. ("Dame" because she had been honored for past achievements; I never knew what.) She had one eye that drooped and was somewhat frightening to the ten-year-old that I was. However, she was also very wise, and kind without being sentimental.

She took one look at me and said, in such a way that I have never forgotten it, "Beware of fear."

It took me many years to understand the power and importance of that observation.

Fear can be one of the most destructive of human emotions. It is, of course, also very important, in that fear sometimes stops you from doing stupid things. But it can also stop you from doing creative or exciting or experimental things. It can cloud your judgment of others, and lead to all kinds of evil. The control and understanding of our personal fears is one of the most important undertakings of our lives.

Arianna Huffington

Bestselling Author and President and Editor in Chief
of the Huffington Post Media Group

―――――

A Lot of Greek Chutzpah

My mother was a continual source of wisdom and great advice. She used to say, "Angels fly because they take themselves lightly." And she taught me that there is always a way around a problem—you've just got to find it. Keep trying doors; one will eventually open. She also taught me to accept failure as part and parcel of life. It's not the opposite of success; it's an integral part of success.

I talk a lot about learning to become fearless in your approach to life. But fearlessness is not the absence of fear. It's the mastery of fear. It's all about getting up one more time than you fall down. I had this lesson brought home to me in a very powerful way in my mid-twenties when I was writing my second book. My first book, *The Female Woman,* had been a surprise success. Instead of accepting any of the book contracts I had been offered to write on women again, I decided to tackle a subject I'd been preoccupied with through college (and, indeed, remain preoccupied with today): the role of leaders in shaping our world. I locked myself in my London apartment and worked around the clock on this book. I would write until I couldn't stay awake—sometimes into the early hours of the morning.

The book was finally finished, and I don't remember ever before or since having been as happy with the work I'd done. So imagine my surprise when publisher after publisher rejected it. Indeed, thirty-six publishers turned it down before it was finally published. It was the kind of rejection that unleashed all kinds of self-doubt, including fears that I was not only on the wrong career path but was going to go broke in the process. "What if the success of my first book was a fluke and I wasn't really meant to be a writer?" I would ask myself in the middle of many a sleepless night. And this was not just a theoretical question—it was also a crassly financial one: "How am I going to pay my bills?" I had used the royalties from my first book to subsidize the second, and now that money was running out. It seemed I had no choice but to get some kind of "real" job.

But my desire to write turned out to be stronger than my fear of poverty. Had I been afraid, I might have tossed the manuscript in the wastebasket somewhere around rejection letter number fifteen and taken a job that had nothing to do with my passion. Instead, I walked into Barclays Bank in St. James's Square in London and met with a banker named Ian Bell. With nothing more to offer than a lot of Greek chutzpah, I asked him for a loan. And, with a lot of unfounded trust, he gave it to me.

I've always been grateful to Ian Bell, and have since sent him a Christmas card every year. He was, after all, the person who made it possible for me to write a book that, though never a commercial success, did finally get published and garnered lots of good reviews. More important, the book was like a seed planted in my twenties that finally sprouted in my forties, when I became seriously engaged in political life.

I had abundant passion and abundant hope (not to mention abundant nerve!), all of which pushed me past all my fears.

David L. Calhoun

Chairman and CEO of the Nielsen Company

Develop Your Own Brand of Self-Confidence

I worked for a guy named Jack Welch for twenty years at GE. He was and is a great mentor and a great leader. If I had to isolate the subject he spoke most passionately to me about during those years, it is that self-confidence is the most important characteristic of successful people. Self-confidence—a quiet self-confidence that is not cockiness, not conceit, not arrogance—is the key to excelling, no matter what you do in life.

Henry David Thoreau once said, "The mass of men lead lives of quiet desperation." I don't believe that most do, but I do believe that quietly desperate people are the ones who never quite found their self-confidence. So how do you get it? What is the secret to developing your own brand of self-confidence?

First, you must resolve to grow intellectually, morally, technically, and professionally every day through your entire work and family life. You need to be absolutely paranoid about the currency of your knowledge, and to ask yourself every day, Am I really up to speed? Or am I stagnating intellectually, faking it or, even worse, falling behind? Am I still learning? Or am I just doing the same stuff on a different day, or, as Otis Redding sings, "sittin' on the dock of the bay / Watching the tide roll away"?

The lust for learning is age-independent. When I worked for GE, we had fifty-five- and sixty-year-old engineers in our jet-engine business who were as leading-edge as anyone I knew then, or have known since. Their lust for learning defined their very being at work and in their communities. They perfected the habit of learning, and they practiced it every working hour despite the fact that many of them were already the world's leading experts in their respective fields. In contrast, we'd occasionally find a thirty-year-old tiptoeing around who had already forgotten how to learn; who may have actually listened to someone who told him, "Today marks the end of learning and the time to begin doing." If you bring that mind-set to companies like GE or Nielsen, your career will be short-lived. We compensate people for what we believe they will learn—for the discoveries that lie ahead—not for yesterday's news.

Next, get to know yourself. Evaluate your strengths and weaknesses with cool objectivity. Even as your confidence grows, you must suppress your ego; focus on your weaknesses and on ways to overcome them. What are your sources of anxiety?

Years ago, still early in my career, I realized that I had no real experience with customers—a shortcoming that caused me great personal anxiety, particularly in light of my boss's desire to promote me quickly into business leadership. Against the advice of my boss, I accepted a job and a demotion in order to work in sales. I've never made a better career move in my life. My confidence grew and my anxiety abated. At another period, I found myself envious of the courage and resourcefulness of GE executives who had spent years in developing markets in Southeast Asia or in South America, where there were strange languages and business practices, different timelines and ways of getting things done. In order to have these experiences, I uprooted my family, with their consent, and took a job in Asia. I faced the unknown, made more than a few mistakes, and am better for it in the end, and so is my family.

During the course of our lives, we must all wrestle with the "work/life balance." This issue, at its heart, comes down once again to self-confidence. Five short years after graduating from college, I fell into a terrible rut, hanging around the office twelve and fourteen hours a day. It was a habit I developed after joining GE's Corporate Audit staff. I routinely found myself getting home well after the kids had fallen asleep. Then I took a job working for a GE vice-chairman named Larry Bossidy. I quickly noticed a few things about Larry, who retired as the CEO of Honeywell. Larry came to work at a reasonable time and left in time for dinner, even if there was the ever-present possibility that Jack

Welch might try to track him down in the evening. By the time I started working for him, he had nine children. He actually knew their names, and he went to a fair number of their games and school functions. Yet, if you surveyed the GE leadership team at any time during Larry's tenure, they would tell you that Larry got more done than anyone they had ever known.

Larry has, and I hope I now have, the self-confidence to let achievements rather than time spent in the office define our value. Nothing on earth can replace my oldest daughter's volleyball games, my other daughter's concerts, my son's hockey games, or coaching my youngest daughter's basketball team . . . nothing on earth!

There is one final attribute of self-confidence: knowing that you possess absolute, unbending, unimpeachable integrity. Everyone must know that—above all else—it is integrity that defines character. There may come a day in your career when you are asked to approve, or wink at, or ignore something that, if you go along with it, will have a positive impact on some measure or metric for which you, your institution, or your friends will be judged favorably. You may know, that day, that you and your colleagues are near the edge. The lawyers or compliance people may say it's "Okay" or "it shouldn't be a problem," or "that's the way they do business in China" or "Hungary" or "in the insurance industry," or wherever. But maybe it just doesn't sit quite right in your gut. It is not the way of global business. You must understand that when you are near the edge, that line in the sand—or that line in your soul—is moving closer to you, not farther away; that you must have the confidence and the courage to say, "No, we are not doing this."

Then you can go home, look your family in the eye, and sleep like a baby. And there is nothing more important in any career than the ability to do that.

George Lopez
Comedian and Host of *Lopez Tonight*

Fortune Favors the Bold

Anyone familiar with my stand-up routine or the show I had on ABC for four years probably knows that I had a miserable childhood. My migrant-worker father took off when I was two months old, and my mixed-up mother abandoned me when I was ten. I was raised by my biological grandmother and her second husband in a poor section of Los Angeles's San Fernando Valley.

Going to college never crossed my mind. Instead, I have a Ph.D. from the school of hard knocks. To the parents of the kids I grew up around, I was an example: "You wanna end up like George Lopez?"

My friends ran faster and were better athletes. And they had parents.

Everything frightened me—the dark, other people, anything new.

But I had two things nobody realized. One was determination. The other was a wicked sense of humor. From as far back as I can remember, something funny would always pop into my head. It was how I dealt with not having as much as everyone else. It has been the one constant companion on my journey.

My grandmother Benita Gutierrez was the inspiration for my ABC show, which featured a dysfunctional family. I can still hear her scolding me: *"Come over here. Why you crying?"* With my grandmother, it wasn't tough love. She was just tough.

My grandmother and the man I called my grandfather, Refugio Gutierrez, were never diligent about my whereabouts or concerned with what I was learning or how I was learning. They never mentioned anything about me going to college or pursuing my education.

Whenever something got tough for me, I quit. And whenever I got upset with someone I avoided that person, which is a form of quitting. I would never say "Sorry," because I never heard the word in my house. All I heard was *"Hey, you, get over it."*

It wasn't healthy to be always quitting. I was only hurting myself. When golf got tough, I quit. When accordion got tough, I quit. When school got tough, I took easier classes. And school was tough for me. I didn't realize it at the time, but I was dyslexic. I didn't know it until my daughter Mayan, now fifteen, was diagnosed with dyslexia when she was five. By then, I was up and successful, so I didn't get treated for it because I didn't want to mess with a formula that was working.

I wasn't a very good student. I graduated from San Fernando High in 1979, with a 2.2 grade-point average. That's why my production company is called 2.2 Production. Growing up, I spent a lot of time at home alone in front of a television set. Freddie Prinze, Sr., became my first idol. When I was a sophomore in high school, I was devastated by the news that he had committed suicide.

Freddie Prinze, more than anyone else, got me interested in comedy. He was responsible for my wanting to become a stand-up comedian.

I got a few gigs in a small comedy club in Westwood after I graduated from high school. It didn't go well. My first stand-up was on June 4, 1979. I was scared to death. I had a wino buy me a small bottle of wine to settle my nerves. It only helped a little.

My second stand-up didn't go very well, either. But the third time was the charm. The audience was laughing, actually laughing. It gave me a feeling I had never experienced before, an infusion of excitement. In fact, I have never felt like that since, with the exception of the day my daughter was born.

The fact that I had actually made people laugh didn't exactly jump-start my career as a stand-up comedian. I had some successes but was often left feeling humiliated. In 1982, I quit. Yes, I quit again.

I had some menial, go-nowhere jobs.

The moment that turned my life around came at 6:15 on the morning of April 23, 1984, my twenty-third birthday. I was sleeping on a friend's couch in a duplex in Pacoima. I realized for the first time that I was going nowhere and that I was not prepared for anything.

I had been battling my disability, battling my desire. I was battling making choices and commitments. It was on that day that I realized I had quit at everything. I made a vow never to give up on stand-up again.

I realized if I didn't take the initiative and rewire myself I would end up being like so many people I knew who never committed themselves to anything and just took any job they could get and stayed there forever.

For the first time, I was determined to trust myself and accept the good as well as the bad as it came. In the back of my mind, I had always felt that I could be somebody. The movie *Rocky* came out when I was in high school, and I said to myself, "That's me."

I had to deal with my fear, my nerves, and my shyness, but I was determined to make it as a stand-up comedian.

The best advice I ever got came in the early 1990s during a comedy festival in San Antonio. That advice was: "Be bold!"

From that point on, I approached everything with a newfound bravado.

There is not a day that goes by that I don't think about how fortunate I am to be doing something that I love, and that as a performer I created a place that previously didn't exist for Latinos. That's important to me.

The message I want to convey is: Be bold. Don't be afraid. Trust your instincts. If you quit, you'll never find out what could have happened. So be yourself, and remember: *Fortune favors the bold!*

Maria Shriver

Award-Winning Journalist, Bestselling Author,
and Former First Lady of California

———

Don't Be Afraid of Being Afraid

Someone once told me not to be afraid of being afraid, because, as she said, "Anxiety is a glimpse of your own daring." Isn't that great? It means that part of your agitation is just excitement about what you're getting ready to accomplish.

Don't sell yourself short by being so afraid of failure that you don't dare to make any mistakes. Make your mistakes and learn from them. And remember: No matter how many mistakes you make, your mother always loves you!

Susan Stroman

Broadway Director and Choreographer

What's the Worst That Could Happen?

As a little girl growing up in Wilmington, Delaware, whenever I found myself in a conundrum I looked to my father for advice. And always he offered the same encouragement: "Ask yourself, what's the worst that could happen? Someone might tell you no, but there's no harm in that." Just take a chance. Ask the question.

When I was struggling to establish myself as a choreographer in New York City, I had an idea, along with my friend Scott Ellis, that we should approach the legendary composing team of John Kander and Fred Ebb about staging a revival of their show *Flora the Red Menace*. Between us we had no money and not many credits, but I knew the idea was a good one. We just needed that "One Good Break"! So, with my father's advice in my ear, we met the famous Kander and Ebb and asked the question.

They said yes.

With Kander and Ebb's blessing, we then took our idea Off Broadway to the Vineyard Theatre in hopes that the company would produce it.

Again, the answer was yes.

I'm here because I took that chance, because I knocked on Kander and Ebb's door and didn't let the fear of rejection stop me from asking. If you really believe in yourself and your art, then you have to create your own opportunities. You can't wait for someone else to do it for you.

Our tiny production of *Flora the Red Menace* opened in 1987. Now, decades later, with many Broadway shows under my belt, I'm once again with Kander and Ebb. Together we just opened the new musical

The Scottsboro Boys on Broadway. I believe in serendipity, but I also believe there are times when you have to be the one who lines up everything so it can fall into place. So just ask the question. After all, what's
the worst that could happen? "No" isn't really so bad, and "Yes" might
take you places you'd never expect.

Tony Hsieh

*#1 New York Times bestselling author of Delivering Happiness
and CEO of Zappos.com, Inc.*

Be Lucky

At Zappos, we try to hire the luckier job candidates. In fact, one of our interview questions is "On a scale from 1 to 10, how lucky are you in life?"

Many years ago, I read about a study in which researchers posed that same question to a random group of people. Each participant was then handed a newspaper and asked to count the number of photos inside. What the participants didn't know was that it was actually a fake newspaper. Sprinkled throughout were headlines such as, "If You're Reading This, the Answer is 37. Collect $100."

Researchers found that the participants who considered themselves unlucky in life generally never noticed the headlines. They diligently completed the assigned task and eventually came up with the answer. But the people who considered themselves lucky in life? They generally stopped early and made an extra hundred dollars.

The takeaway here is not so much about being inherently lucky or unlucky in life. Rather, luck is more about being open to opportunities beyond how the task or situation presents itself.

So try to be more creative, more adventurous, and more open-minded as you go about your life. Try to notice opportunities in disguise. Try to think more outside the box.

In short?

Be lucky.

PART 2

THE BANK OF EXPERIENCE

On Hard Work and Tenacity

I'm a great believer in luck, and I find the harder I work, the more I have of it.　　　　　　　　　　　　　—Thomas Jefferson

I n April of 2009, I had the privilege of interviewing Captain Chesley "Sully" Sullenberger, the pilot who landed that incapacitated US Airways flight on the Hudson River after geese had knocked out both engines. Sully's split-second judgment and calm demeanor that winter day saved all one hundred fifty-five passengers and crew members on board. While his story is about grace under pressure, it's also about the value of hard work and the importance of logging enough hours that the expertise you've built up almost goes on autopilot. "For forty-two years," he told me, "I've been making small, regular deposits in this bank of experience. And on January 15th the balance was sufficient so that I could make a sudden, large withdrawal."

Success really is ten percent inspiration and ninety percent perspiration. As Malcolm Gladwell wrote in his now famous book *Outliers,* to truly master something you need to spend at least ten thousand hours doing it. One example he cites: the Fab Four. The Beatles might have seemed like an overnight sensation, but they had played together more than a thousand times before that famous appearance on *The Ed Sullivan Show* back in 1964. For them, it really was a hard day's night—night after night after night for years! Bill Gates's birthday set him up perfectly for the technical revolution that was taking hold in this country, but good timing wasn't everything. He dropped out of Harvard and spent every waking moment building and understanding computer codes.

There is simply no way around it. There is no substitute for hard work. Early in my career and to this day, I've put in as many hours as needed to get the job done. If it meant working after hours, on weekends, in the middle of the night and getting two hours of sleep, I would do it. People notice. They also notice when you're doing the bare minimum. Nothing is less appealing in a work setting than a fresh-out-of-college graduate, who's entitled and unmotivated. If you're the low man or woman on the totem pole, learn from those up at or close to the top. Pick their brains, follow them around. They'll probably be flattered. Even today, I'm still learning from my colleagues. When I see an interview or a story that I really like, I'll watch it several times to understand what made it so good.

No matter how many hours you put in, or how much sweat equity you amass, there will be times when you feel you aren't getting the credit you deserve or promotion you've earned. You will inevitably face disappointments. One of the most empowering lessons of all is: Life isn't fair. This is something I tried to teach my daughters. When they were demanding toddlers, I often responded to their whines by telling them, "Girls, you know what Mick Jagger says: 'You can't always get what you want.'" If you realize that disappointment will always be part of the equation, regardless of how unfair it feels, your recovery time will be much faster.

And sometimes things just don't go your way because someone beats you fair and square. I remember I was desperate to profile Chris Reeves following his horseback-riding accident, because he was one of the most inspiring people I'd ever met. I was relentless. I called his representative almost every day. I wrote letters. Called some more. When I found out that Barbara Walters was going to do a one-hour special on Chris and his wife, Dana, I was crestfallen. But my disappointment was quickly defused when I realized that he had a long-standing relationship with Barbara and, after so many impressive years in the business, why wouldn't he turn to her and trust her? I watched the special, which was beautifully done. And I thought to myself: This was the right decision. I also thought about a famous line by media mogul Barry Diller: "I lost. She won. Next."

Sometimes hard work and good timing intersect. Sometimes they don't. But they likely will at some point, and when they do, like Sully . . . you'll be ready.

Apolo Ohno

Speed Skater and Eight-Time Medalist in the Winter Olympics

It's Not About the Forty Seconds

My dad always used to tell me that sometimes you have to have a massive storm in order to clear the sky. Whenever it rains like crazy one day, the next day will be filled with sunshine, a clear blue sky, and everything will be pristine. To me, that's what life's journey is all about. You have to be willing to put forth the dedication and effort to go through the storms; to be the one out there putting in the time and the work in order to enjoy what could be waiting at the end when the air clears.

But there's a hitch: There's no guarantee that you're going to reach your goal—that's the thing. It's not really about the destination, but about what it took to get you there. After I've crossed the finish line in a race, I sometimes think to myself, Oh my gosh, the past four years of my life have been dedicated to a race that lasted only forty seconds. You know, I can't remember the forty seconds in their entirety, but I can remember a lot more about the bulk of time leading up to the race when I was training. I think that's a very useful perspective to have. It's not about the forty seconds; it's about the four years, the time it took to get there. So that destination point no longer becomes the true focal point. It becomes a goal, it gives me a point to focus on, but in terms of overall importance it's not very significant. The things that I learned about myself and what I endured throughout those four years are really what mattered most.

The 2002 and 2010 Olympic Games both had many instances in which I was the strongest, the fastest, the most fit, and also the skater with the best strategy, but something happened and I didn't come in first. Either I slipped or somebody bumped me—something seemingly out of my control happened—and I didn't win the race. I complained to myself—*Man, that kinda sucked*—because I felt that I was the best person yet I didn't win. But in the end it wasn't really about the win or the loss.

In 2002, I weighed about 165 pounds and I leg-pressed approximately 1,400 pounds. In 2006, I weighed 157 pounds and leg-pressed about 1,500 pounds—my strength-to-weight ratio was a lot higher. Four years later, in 2010, I vowed to weigh less than 150 pounds. I wanted to race at 147, so I had to totally change my mentality about what was possible from a physical perspective. To put that into context, I hadn't raced under 150 pounds since I was fourteen years old, and here I was going to be almost twenty-eight. I ended up racing at 141 pounds and leg-pressing almost 2,000 pounds, so that to me was a testament to the strength of my mind and my will. You can accomplish whatever you set out to do, even when people think it can't be done. As an athlete, that's what taught me most about myself. It was more about the training and the discipline that led up to the race rather than about the race itself. Even now, looking back on that training, I think, Wow, I actually did it. That was pretty cool.

Chelsea Handler

Stand-Up Comedian, Bestselling Author, and Television Host

Pay Attention!

I wish someone had told me when I was growing up that succeeding in life is as simple as paying attention. Paying attention to everything and everyone, and not just paying attention to Lifetime movies starring Tiffani Amber Thiessen and Emmanuel Lewis, and reruns of *Charles in Charge,* wishing it would turn into a reality show called *Chelsea in Charge.* Paying attention to each person's success and each person's failure, and learning that the two go hand in hand. Paying attention to the fact that just when you think everything's going your way, it won't, and just when you're ready to give up you'll be reminded of why you started trying in the first place.

If someone had told me that I'd be able to make a living by hiring a bunch of my friends, throwing food at them on a daily basis, and then spending half an hour making fun of celebrities, I would have dropped out of kindergarten. You can do whatever you want to do—you can create a job that never existed, you can create nonsense or create genius. But as long as you're paying attention you'll grab inspiration from everything and create something that's a little different and a little newer. If you're really lucky, you'll end up being the first woman to anchor the evening news by herself, or the first woman to anchor a show on the E! network. Just pay attention. And, no matter what, don't sleep with your boss.

Michael Bloomberg

108th Mayor of New York City and Founder of Bloomberg, L.P.

The Real Eighty Percent

Woody Allen once said that "eighty percent of success is showing up." But I'd like to amend that. I think eighty percent of success is showing up . . . *early.* Let me explain.

When I was in business school, I worked a summer job in a real-estate office renting apartments. Four full-time professional brokers worked there, but every day the majority of customers who came in seemed to have an appointment with me—the kid! The others could never figure it out, but all I did was come in early and answer the phone. My calendar was full by the time they arrived at 9 A.M. That summer I made enough money to pay room, board, and tuition for my whole second year at business school. (I don't think I was the first one in the classroom each morning, but that's another story.)

I took the same approach at my first job after business school. Toiling at the bottom of the ladder at Salomon Brothers, the Wall Street firm, I made sure that I was the first one in the office every day. Not only did it save me a little money, by allowing me to read the office copy of *The Wall Street Journal,* it also gave me the chance to get to know the other guy who was always there before everyone else: the CEO, Billy Salomon.

Of course, even with hard work there will be setbacks. After fifteen years, I was fired from Salomon, a company I loved. But the following day I went to work starting a technology company with three guys, one coffeepot, and no customers. It was a major risk, and most people tried to talk me out of it. With a lot of long hours and hard work, the company grew, and its success eventually gave me the chance to run for mayor of New York City—another long shot that most people thought I was crazy to attempt. And maybe I was. But I've never feared failure or hard work. That approach—along with a lot of luck—has opened doors I never imagined possible. And I still try to walk through those doors every morning before anyone else.

Jeff Immelt

CEO of General Electric

Be Humbled by What You Don't Know

One of my great lessons of leadership is the knowledge that no task is beneath me. In 1989, I was leading GE's appliance service business when we had a catastrophic failure of our refrigerators and had to replace three million compressors. Despite my lofty title, I learned how to fix compressors. I would go out into people's homes to do this so that I could understand the problem. For a math major, there is no better way to be humbled than to sit on someone's kitchen floor while the ice cream melts. I didn't have to do this, but I can't tell you how much I learned. In 1997, I was leading our health-care division. We wanted to build a business in China, and our sales were close to zero. I didn't want to merely read a book about China, and our local team didn't know GE. So I spent three weeks in China and visited two hundred hospitals in twenty-five cities with the local team. At the end, we designed a product line and a distribution process. Today, the company has a billion-dollar health-care business in China that can satisfy every segment of the population. I didn't have to do this, but it helped me understand the Chinese culture.

In 2004, we studied global warming in order to understand the science behind it, its impact on our customers, and whether we could develop technical solutions. Despite the fact that I had 300,000 people working for me, I wanted to develop my own sense for the issues. I spent my entire vacation studying technical reports and speaking with experts. I couldn't delegate the analysis; I wanted to own it. I didn't have to do this, but my firsthand knowledge is better because

I did. I am humbled by what I don't know. But I have a passion for learning. I want to learn things on my own terms. I enjoy common tasks, and I know that no job is beneath me. When you are willing to learn, and get your hands dirty and be accountable, people will follow.

Donald J. Trump
Chairman and President of the Trump Organization

Know Everything You Can

My father told me, "Know everything you can about what you're doing." He was my mentor, and I spent time working with him and watching him for many years. He had a comprehensive approach to his work and his life, and I learned a lot from being around him. What he told me in that short sentence had great significance as I grew up and became a businessman myself. I understand now how important it is to be thorough and well prepared in daily life. It has to do with focus; without focus, things can become difficult as well as unproductive. So know everything you can about what you're doing—which is a daily commitment to education, excellence, and persistence.

Ellen Johnson Sirleaf

Twenty-fourth President of Liberia

No Job Is Small

In instilling the value of menial work in me and my siblings while we were very young, our mother always said, "Only sin cannot be removed through washing with water and soap." This became a part of our culture, making it easy for me as a wife and mother in mid-career to take on the job as waiter and cleaner in the Rennebohn Drug Store near the campus of the University of Wisconsin–Madison.

Jimmy Carter
Thirty-ninth President of the United States and
Founder of the Carter Center

Always Do Your Best

One of the most formative moments in my life was when I first met Navy Admiral Hyman Rickover. Admiral Rickover was a remarkable man who had a profound effect on my life—perhaps more than anyone except my parents.

In 1949, because of the admiral's prodding, the Navy made a commitment to developing a nuclear-propulsion plant for ships, and then contracted with two major companies to build prototype atomic-powered submarines. I had applied for the nuclear-submarine program, and Admiral Rickover was interviewing me for the job.

We sat in a large room by ourselves for more than two hours, and he let me choose any subject I wished to discuss. Very carefully, I chose those about which I knew most at the time—current events, seamanship, music, literature, naval tactics, electronics, gunnery—and he began to ask me a series of questions. In each instance, he soon proved that I knew relatively little about the subject I had chosen.

He always looked right into my eyes, and he never smiled. I was saturated with cold sweat. Finally, he asked me a question, and I thought I could redeem myself.

He said, "How did you stand in your class at the Naval Academy?"

Since I had completed my sophomore year at Georgia Tech before entering Annapolis as a plebe, I had done very well, and my chest swelled with pride as I answered, "Sir, I stood fifty-ninth in a class of eight hundred and twenty!"

I sat back to wait for the congratulations, which never came. Instead, the admiral asked, "Did you do your best?"

I started to say, "Yes, sir," but I remembered who this was, and recalled several of the many times at the academy when I could have learned more about our allies, our enemies, weapons, strategy, and so forth. I was just human. I finally gulped and said, "No, sir, I didn't always do my best."

He looked at me for a long time, and then turned his chair around to end the interview. He asked one final question, which I have never been able to forget—or to answer. He said, "Why not?" I sat there for a while, shaken, and then slowly left the room.

But I did get the job.

As I got to know Admiral Rickover, I came to admire how unbelievably hardworking and competent he was. He demanded total dedication from his subordinates. We feared and respected him and strove to please him. I do not in that period remember his ever saying a complimentary word to me. The absence of a comment was his compliment; he never hesitated to criticize severely if a job wasn't done as well as he believed it could be done. He expected the maximum from us, but he always contributed more.

My job was the best and most promising in the Navy, and the work was challenging and worthwhile. The salary was good, and the retirement benefits were liberal and assured. But the contact with Admiral Rickover alone made it worthwhile.

Larry King

Emmy Award–Winning Television and Radio Host

———

Learn How to Listen

I never learned anything when I was talking. The best learning lesson I can give you on accomplishment is to listen. Learn how to listen. You don't learn anything when you are talking. Think about it.

Muhtar Kent

Chairman and CEO of the Coca-Cola Company

In Good Times and in Bad

Relationships work only when you're there for people in tough times as well as the good. Let me give you a real case in point.

In 1989, at the age of thirty-six, I was appointed president of Coca-Cola's East Central European division. It was my responsibility to orchestrate Coca-Cola's entry into the former Soviet Union and Eastern Europe after the fall of the Berlin Wall. The region included twenty-three countries where 350 million people had lived literally behind a wall for as much as seventy years. Basic democratic concepts like human rights, free speech, free enterprise, and land ownership were all novelties.

Coca-Cola had zero existing infrastructure in the region. No bottling plants. No distribution systems. The challenge for us was to set up more than twenty plants and a modern distribution system in mere months, across twenty-three nations.

Albania at that time was one of the most politically and economically isolated nations in the world. Its economy was in shambles and its people were in great need. We saw potential there and were determined to open a bottling facility in the country. My team and I knew that we needed to find the right people to help us. One day, an acquaintance pointed a doctor out to me, saying, "You should meet this man."

I found the doctor in his office. The room had no heating, and his patients sat on wooden fruit boxes. Over the next few months, I developed a relationship with him and would send him copies of Western newspapers and periodicals. One year later, during the first free elections, this doctor—Sali Berisha—became the first elected president of Albania.

Coca-Cola became the country's first foreign investment, and in 1993 we opened the first modern Coca-Cola plant in the region.

Today, Coca-Cola directly and indirectly employs more than two thousand people in Albania; the country is thriving, and we are the undisputed market leader. It just goes to show the wisdom behind that time-tested adage that encourages us all to work together in good times and in bad. When you stand behind someone or something, no matter how daunting the task or how hard the circumstances, the result can be truly amazing.

Ryan Seacrest

Radio Personality, Television Host, and Producer

———

The Hardest-Working Guy in Showbiz

There's a mantra I've lived by throughout my entire career that I think is one of the keys to my success: *Say yes.* Accept the job, agree to that meeting, catch up over a cup of coffee, lend a helping hand. You never know what the future will bring, so always make the best use of the present. I often get teased for having so many jobs and such a busy schedule, but, truthfully, seizing each of these opportunities has led to many others. And remember, you can always say no later—or so I've heard.

Robin Roberts

Emmy Award–Winning Television Broadcaster, Journalist, and Co-Host of *Good Morning America*

Determination Makes the Difference

When I was young, I was totally focused on being an athlete. It taught me invaluable life lessons. During my freshman year at Southeastern Louisiana University, my basketball coach, Linda Puckett, devised a challenging drill. She instructed my teammates and me to stay in a crouched position as we slid around the perimeter of the court. Despite the burn in our thighs and our trembling calf muscles, we weren't supposed to stand up until we reached the end point. I was in the middle of the pack as we did the drill. When we were finished, Coach Puckett got right in my face and said, "Hon, you are going places in life." Turns out I was the only one who remained crouched in that uncomfortable position for the entire time. It took discipline, determination, and stamina—traits that come in handy in life. Be patient and persistent. Life is not so much what you accomplish as what you overcome.

Steven Spielberg
Academy Award–Winning Director and Producer

Listen and Learn

From a very young age, my parents taught me the most important lesson of my whole life: They taught me how to listen. They taught me how to listen to everybody before I made up my own mind. When you listen, you learn. You absorb like a sponge—and your life becomes so much better than when you are just trying to be listened to all the time.

PART 3

NEVER GIVE IN

On Pluck and Perseverance

When you come to the end of your rope, tie a knot and hang on.

—FRANKLIN D. ROOSEVELT

I could probably write an entire book about the people who thought I'd never make it in television. I guess I'll begin at the beginning. In the early eighties, when I was working at CNN as an assistant assignment editor, the Washington bureau chief, Stuart Loory, decided to give me my first big break. He approached me one day and said, "Katie, would you like to go to the White House every morning and report on the president's schedule for the day?" I could hardly believe it. I had never done a TV report in my life, and now I was going to be at the White House! I went home, thrilled and terrified, spent much of the evening in front of the mirror, talking earnestly into my hairbrush, and had a sleepless night fantasizing about my acclaimed television debut. The next morning, the crew helped me put in my earpiece and watched as showtime approached. During the commercial break, I heard the two anchors Dave Walker and Lois Hart, a married couple, chatting with each other. "Who is that girl?" Lois asked. "I don't know," Dave answered. "But she looks like she's about sixteen years old!" Confidence began to escape my body like air from a tire. When they "threw" to me, I recited the president's schedule in a singsongy voice, more or less reading from the AP wire: "At ten o'clock, the president has a meeting with National Security Adviser Zbigniew Brzezinski"—working a tad too hard to pronounce it properly. When it was over, more relieved than anything else, I went back to the bureau, where a very nice assignment editor named Bill Hensel told me that he had gotten a call from the president of CNN, Reese Schonfeld. The message was blunt: He never wanted to see me on the air again.

I eventually started doing some reporting, thanks to another, much more encouraging on-air married couple named Don Farmer and Chris Curle. I had first met Don when he was a correspondent for *20/20* at ABC News and had knocked on his office door armed with a list of potential story ideas. Our paths crossed again a couple of years later at CNN when I moved to Atlanta to produce Don and Chris's show. They thought I had potential and allowed me to do some reporting. My on-air presentation improved and I was offered a job as a local reporter for the CBS affiliate in Miami. Two years later, I was hired by WRC, the NBC affiliate in Washington, D.C. While I was there, I asked my news director if I could anchor the morning cut-ins, the short local news updates that ran twenty-five minutes after the hour during the *Today* show. He was skeptical but agreed to let me try. As Yogi Berra said, it was déjà vu all over again. I was expected to write the copy, edit, and time the accompanying video, and run my own teleprompter. I was terrible. I continued talking long after the computer had automatically triggered the commercial break. I'm sure the age-old expression "deer in the headlights" was dusted off to describe my performance. When I saw said news director later that day, I asked if I could anchor the local cut-ins another time, knowing my first foray was, um, subpar. "Sure," he told me. "If you go to a really, really, really small market somewhere." It was, in short, another disaster.

So why didn't I just throw in the towel and say, "Maybe I'm not cut out for this business"? I knew that my skills needed to be honed and that I was a work-in-progress, but I was convinced that I had the skills and could do the job. I also knew something else. Along the way, you're bound to encounter people who are naysayers and buzz killers. Maybe they're insecure, maybe they're bitter, maybe they simply lack imagination. Those people need to be strained from your life like sand from a colander of freshly washed seashells. But then again, some of them may—*surprise!*—be right. Sure, they could have been more tactful, but both of my hypercritical news directors—men who in so many words told me, "You can't"—actually did me a favor. I worked harder, got better, and became more determined than ever to prove them wrong.

About six months after my disastrous morning cut-in debut, I had started working at NBC as a Pentagon correspondent. During Christmas, management was desperate to find someone to fill in for Garrick Utley on the Saturday *Nightly News.* They asked me. Having practiced over and over with a prompter, I got through the broadcast without hyperventilating. When I saw my former news director in the hallway of the building that NBC shared with WRC, I reminded him about telling me to go to a really, really, really small market somewhere to read the cut-ins. "Well," I said teasingly, "is the entire nation a small enough market for you?" He hates that story. But really, he who shall not be named deserves only this: Thank you. To paraphrase Jack Nicholson in *As Good as It Gets,* he made me want to be a better broadcaster. And I did get better. (Thank God.)

Drew Brees

Quarterback for the New Orleans Saints

Use Adversity as an Opportunity

There are many times when an event will happen in your life, something heartbreaking or tragic, and the immediate human response is to ask why. "Why me? Why now? This is the worst thing that has ever happened to me." We have all had those moments. And, however trivial they seem now, when we look back on them, at the time they were devastating. I can remember one of these moments as if it was yesterday. It changed the course of my career and my life. At the time, I thought it was the worst thing that could ever happen to me, and I asked myself all those "why" questions. It was December 31, 2005. I was the quarterback for the San Diego Chargers, playing in the last game of the season, and approaching an off-season where I did not have a contract moving forward. Things were looking up, though, as I envisioned signing a long-term deal with San Diego that would keep me there my entire career. Midway through the second quarter, that all changed in the blink of an eye. I dropped back to pass, only to be blindsided and to watch as the ball fumbled out of my hands onto the ground. I jumped in the pile along with a few defenders to try and recover the ball, only to emerge seconds later with a dislocated throwing shoulder. This is the worst injury a QB can have. Our livelihood is throwing the football, and with a shoulder out of socket this becomes impossible. I saw the doctor a few days later, and he confirmed my worst fears: I had a very serious shoulder injury that would take eight months to heal properly if I was lucky, and it might be two years before I felt totally normal again. Some doctors even gave me a twenty-five-percent chance of ever playing again after seeing the injury up close.

So, with my future in San Diego gone and my football career in serious jeopardy, I was faced with a choice. I could sit and feel sorry for myself or I could use this adversity as an opportunity: an opportunity to bring my shoulder back not only as good as but better than it was before. This injury had happened to me for a reason, I thought, and although I may not see it now, it will be for the better. I just need to trust and have faith and believe that if I do things the right way good things will happen. What is meant to be will happen for me, and all I should concern myself with is the things I can control.

Two months later, in the midst of my rehabilitation, I received a call from the New Orleans Saints asking if I would consider being their QB. They were one of only two teams that showed any interest. I felt a calling to New Orleans that transcended the game of football. It involved the rebuilding of not only a team and an organization but also a city, a region, and, more so than anything, the rebuilding of a mind-set. I now look at what this great city has accomplished post–Hurricane Katrina and smile. It is hard not to reflect on the circumstances that brought me here. At the time, I thought my shoulder injury was the worst thing that could have happened to me. Now I look back and say it was the best thing that ever happened to me. It brought me to New Orleans and allowed me to be a part of this special journey.

Michelle Kwan
Figure-Skating Champion

Fall Down and Get Back Up

I started figure skating at the age of five, and the first thing my coach taught me was how to fall. I remember gazing up at the coach with a puzzled expression, thinking, Shouldn't I be learning how to skate? Why is she teaching me how to fall? Looking back, I realize that my coach was very smart. She knew that I was bound to fall many times throughout my career and that I'd need to learn how to handle it. And boy was she right! Even at twenty-five, as a world champion, I still fell. A lot.

In 1997, I was the reigning national and world champion. I remember feeling the weight of the world on my shoulders. Instead of my usual "go for it" attitude, I was skating in every competition as if I was afraid to lose. (And when you skate like you're afraid to fall, you usually do fall!) That year, during the U.S. Nationals in Nashville, Tennessee, my worst fears were realized. Although my choreography, music, costume, and even makeup seemed perfect, I was far from perfect that evening when I skated the long program. To this day, I still wince thinking of how many jumps I missed and spills I took. It was truly the worst performance of my career.

It would have been very easy for me to give up that night, right in the middle of the program, but I was determined to get through it. Every time I fell I just picked myself back up and kept going; each fall, each miss, made me even more determined to finish the program. And I did. It wasn't pretty, but I got through it.

That competition taught me to never give up. And it's a lesson I took with me for the rest of my skating career and beyond. Pick yourself up and keep going. As a competitive skater, you win some and you lose some. In the end, your finest moments in life aren't necessarily those in which you finish first but, instead, the times when you know that you simply gave it your best—when you did it heart and soul, and held nothing back.

Christina Applegate
Emmy Award–Winning Actress

You Don't Have the Luxury of Negative Thought

It was March 11, 2005, 8 P.M. The orchestra had just finished the last note before the curtain was to rise on yet another preview performance of *Sweet Charity*. I was in the wings awaiting my cue. I ran out to twirl around the lamppost and deliver my first line: "Ya ever have one of those days that was perfect?" I had done this now for a month, eight shows a week, and all without a hitch. But this night as I twirled an uneven part of the stage caught my heel and I heard a horrible snap. At first there wasn't any pain, and I continued to deliver my line and to prepare for the show's opening song. But as the moments went on the pain became unbearable and I looked down and saw that my foot was broken. There I was in front of twenty-five hundred people, with a broken foot and no way off the stage. It was a devastating blow. I was truly frightened. And all I could think was: I have ruined everything. We had been at this for months—working and rehearsing tirelessly as a cast that had truly become a family. We were one month away from opening on Broadway, in a show that was my dream come true. But now time stopped. We were faced with the fact that the show might not go on....

After scrambling to get my understudy ready to take over the remaining preview shows, I had one task: to heal. But how? How could I do this? The bone was broken in half. And this was a show in which my character didn't leave the stage for two hours. Not to mention it was dance heavy. I needed that foot.

Besides going to many different doctors, most of whom said it was nearly impossible for me to heal before opening night, I called the one person I knew who could help: my longtime friend and teacher, the Reverend Michael Beckwith. After a conversation filled with tears and incredible fear, he said this to me: "You do not have the luxury of negative thought." Uhhh . . . okay. "How can I not have negative thoughts when doctors are telling me I can't do this?" I asked. "And when we are faced with the fact that the show might be forced to close? And that my amazing castmates are about to lose their jobs? Jobs we have all put our hearts and souls into?" Once again he said, "You do not have the luxury of negative thought." I had a job to do! Reverend Beckwith gave me the task of envisioning the bone healing faster than was humanly possible. Of playing over and over in my mind the doctor saying to me, "It's a miracle!" And so I did. Every day I participated in the healing of that bone. I felt those negative thoughts coming through and told them to shove it! I kept my eye focused on the task at hand. I did not have the luxury of negative thought; of listening to the lies we so often tell ourselves; of being talked out of success by my fears. And within two weeks a doctor did say to me, "Wow, I have never seen a bone heal this quickly."

To make a long story short, the show did indeed go on—with Tony nominations and great success. It was the single most rewarding and unforgettable experience of my life, and it changed me forever. Those same words and the power they held would serve me again in 2008, during one of the most challenging periods in my life: when I was diagnosed with cancer. Again, I said to myself, "I do not have the luxury of negative thought! Not when I need to make the impossible oh-so-possible." They are words I live by. And although I occasionally falter and my mind tries to convince me otherwise, it was those words that helped fuse a bone together at record speed. So believe me, this s*** works.

Ken Chenault

Chairman and CEO of American Express

Face History and Make History

My father, Dr. Hortenius Chenault, passed the New York State dental licensing exam in 1939 with the highest score recorded to date. Soon after, with the onset of World War II, he wanted to serve his country by enlisting in the U.S. Army Dental Corps but was turned away. He was black, and the Army Dental Corps was segregated.

This was hardly enough to stop my father. He met and befriended some foreign officers, made a few inquiries, learned to speak French, and then joined the more accommodating European-based Allied Forces Dental Society.

Years later, he would tell me and my brothers and sister, "No one was going to tell me what I could do." He believed that deeply, and he made sure that his children believed it, too. That's why after the war, on Long Island, where we grew up, my father fought to fully integrate the school system. He would not settle for schools where African-American students were automatically put into vocational programs and kept off the academic track.

Nobody was going to tell us what we could do. What we could aspire to. What we could accomplish.

At the dinner table, my brothers and sister would ask my father what we needed to do to make a difference. He would say that progress could be slow and frustrating. And, of course, that could make you angry. But his basic view was that we needed to fight for our rights and concentrate on the things we could control. And what you can control, he would tell us, is your own performance.

As my father taught me, work hard, don't ever let anyone stop you or keep you down, focus on what you can control, and you can accomplish an extraordinary amount.

Matthew McConaughey

Actor, Director, and Creator of the j.k. livin Foundation

You Were Just Having Trouble

Growing up, my dad got mad at me for only two reasons: if I told a lie or if I said "I can't." It was easy to understand the "lying" part, but the "can't" bit took a little longer to figure out.

It was a Saturday morning in the summer of 1981, and I was twelve years old. I was up early to mow the yard so that I could have the afternoon free to play. I got the Snapper lawn mower out of the shed and tried to crank it up. I pulled and pulled the cord, but the lawn mower wasn't turning over. I checked the gas, set the choke, everything I could think of, but I still couldn't get it started. I was exhausted. I was frustrated. I cussed at the mower and at the fresh blister that had formed on my palm from pulling the cord so many times.

My dad came around from the front of the house. I'm not sure how long he was there or if he'd seen me trying to start that damn lawn mower. What I do remember is our conversation. I remember it verbatim. He said, "What's the problem, little man?"

I said, "Dad, I can't get this thing started."

I will never forget the look on his face as he slowly gritted his teeth and said, "You what?"

"I can't get this darn mower started, Dad!"

He looked at me and evenly but sternly said, "No, son, you're having trouble getting that lawn mower started."

I said, "Right, I can't get it—"

"No," he interrupted. "You're *having trouble.*"

"Yes, sir," I said. "What's the difference?"

He said, "Look, son, don't ever say you can't do something. That

------

means there's absolutely no way to do it. If you can't do something, how are you ever gonna fix something? How are you gonna figure the problem out? How are you gonna ask for help? You're gonna have trouble doing a lot of things in life, but they *can* be done. If you say 'I can't,' that means there's no solution, you've given up, you've quit. But if you're 'having trouble,' that means that even though you may not know at the time how to solve the problem, you know there's a way—you're just having trouble. Let's figure it out."

As he knelt down over the lawn mower, he found a loose gas line that was disconnected and wasn't allowing gas to flow to the carburetor. We reconnected it, and after a few pulls the lawn mower started. We shook hands with a smile as I said, "Thanks."

"Sure, little man," he said. "You were just having trouble."

This lesson has stayed with me to this day, and is one I'm passing on to my children. It has helped me work harder, solve problems, and not feel helpless in unfortunate situations. It's given me patience with others and with myself, and, most of all, it leaves the problem open to being solved. Which, of course, always leads to a solution.

Morgan Freeman
Academy Award–Winning Actor

You Quit, You Fail

If I've learned one life-serving lesson, it is that dogged determination pays off. The surest way to lose at any endeavor is to quit.

Once, while sailing in the Windward Islands, I put into Marigot Bay, St. Lucia, needing to replace the water-pump impeller on my diesel engine. After putting ashore by dinghy, I went to the marine store in Rodney Bay, certain of success but not having any. I scoured the town of Castries, canvassing every store and shop that looked as if it might carry an impeller for the Perkins 4-108 diesel engine. I took jitneys and walked most of the day, to no avail. Finally, in late afternoon, tired, sweaty, hungry, and thoroughly discouraged, I sat on a retaining wall and pondered the proverbial end-of-the-rope question: Now what? Then my eyes settled on a large fishing boat tied up in an estuary not fifty yards off the road. I walked over and told the guy on the boat my problem.

"Come on," he said. "I think I know who can help you."

We walked along a dirt path for a short distance, stepped through a chain-link fence, and wound up in someone's yard. Engine parts were everywhere. This was the home of a "shade tree mechanic."

"Perkins 4-108? I believe I do have a couple you can have."

And so he did. Cost: EC$25, about $8.25.

The lesson was clear to me: Don't give up. Fatigue, discomfort, discouragement are merely symptoms of effort. I was on the verge of giving up when salvation was staring me right in the face. Had I not taken that one last walk across the road, I would have failed. There are a lot of incidents like that in my life, but that one was so resonant that I've never forgotten the lesson. You quit, you fail.

Raúl de Molina
Television Personality

———

Against Apparent Odds, Never Give Up

I arrived in the United States at the tender age of sixteen, searching, as so many before me, for the American dream. But the first thing I noticed about my destination—Miami—was how similar it felt to Madrid, where I had lived as a teenager, and Havana, where I was born. Everyone spoke Spanish. Once I'd settled in Miami, my interests proved to be very different from those of your typical Cuban-American teenager. I went from loving soccer and bullfighting to following NASCAR and pro wrestling. Men like Dusty Rhodes, also known as "The American Dream," Abdullah the Butcher, Richard Petty, and Jackie Stewart were my heroes.

In high school, I swiftly became the school's yearbook and newspaper photographer. Later on, after graduating from college, I became a professional photographer. It was during this time that my boss, Phil Sandlin, the photo editor at the Associated Press in Miami, taught me to never give up or take no for an answer. I covered every riot, trial, coup, and other major news event in Miami and Latin America during the 1980s and early 1990s. Never a dull moment. Then came *Miami Vice*, with Don Johnson, and so began an American obsession with celebrity. My focus shifted from news to starlets—I became a celebrity photographer. My photos graced the covers of every major publication, from *The National Enquirer, The Sun* (London), and *The News of the World* to *France Dimanche* and *Hello!* magazine.

I was invited to the set of Joan Rivers's show on numerous occasions to discuss my famous photographs, among them shots of Princess Diana, Princess Caroline of Monaco, Prince Charles, George Michael, Delta Burke, Jane Fonda, Madonna, and many others.

On one of these occasions, a Univision executive happened to see me and, not long afterward, I received an offer to join the network. It was my first foray into Spanish television—a world that was totally foreign to me.

For the past twenty years, I have hosted or co-hosted the most important Hispanic entertainment events in the States: the red carpet for the Latin Grammys, the popular music awards show *Premio lo Nuestro,* and Univision's annual New Year's Eve Show, live from Times Square. For the past twelve years, I have hosted the number-one entertainment news show on Spanish television with Lili Estefan, *El Gordo y la Flaca,* live every day at 4 P.M. Now the celebrity photographers follow me.

Who would have thought all this was possible for a guy who weighs close to three hundred pounds? Since I was a kid, I've always been on the heavy side. By the time I turned seven I was a chubby little boy, but that didn't stop me from playing sports or feeling good about myself. Later, during my high school years, I tipped the scales at over two hundred pounds, but thanks to my gig as yearbook photographer I was extremely popular with the cheerleaders. When I became a news photographer, I ran all over the place without any problems, but I always knew that television would be the ultimate test.

In a world that so often values physical attributes above talent, my weight has posed no problems. Quite the opposite, in fact, perhaps because I never paid much attention to it. The one and only time I have ever felt discriminated against was during my first trip to Hawaii. I took a helicopter tour and was charged double. I got over it.

People en Español named me one of its fifty most beautiful people in America. On another occasion, I made its Best Dressed list, in the excellent company of George Clooney and Ricky Martin. A couple of years ago, I wrote a diet book called *La Dieta del Gordo* (The Fat Guy's Diet), and it became an instant bestseller in the Spanish market. Not bad for a guy most people know as El Gordo.

Tavis Smiley

PBS Host, Author, and Philanthropist

———

Fail Better

"Ever tried. Ever failed. No matter. Try again. Fail again. Fail better."

The words of the great writer and poet Samuel Beckett. Words that I have learned to live by.

Anyone who has ever succeeded in any human endeavor will tell you that he learned more from his failures than he ever learned from his successes. If he's being honest.

But a funny thing happens when "success" becomes an individual's dominant definer. Very few people want to then actually acknowledge the mistakes they've made along the way. That's unfortunate, because it promulgates an artificial concept of "success." By artificial, I mean the notion that people become successful without what I call "success scars." Let's be clear: There is no success without failure. Period. And usually a lot of it.

I used to love Michael Jordan's "Failure" commercial for Nike. You might recall it:

I've missed more than 9,000 shots in my career.
I've lost almost 300 games.
Twenty-six times I've been trusted to take the game-winning shot . . . and missed.
I've failed over and over and over again in my life.
And that is why I succeed.

Powerful stuff.

When you think about it, Beckett was right. Life is ultimately about failing better. Every day that you wake up, you get another chance to get it right. To fail better. We have to learn to think of failure in a different way. To think of failure as a friend, really. A friend who, if embraced, can usher us into new experiences, exposures, and excellencies.

Just look around—there are examples everywhere of people who have failed up. Others have done it, and you can, too.

Valerie Plame

Former United States CIA Operations Officer and Author of *Fair Game*

Life Is Unfair

My father was a career Air Force officer who fought in the South Pacific during World War II. He had a pragmatic approach to life and, growing up, my older brother Robert and I were accustomed to hearing him say, "Life is unfair." My father applied his favorite bit of wisdom to every one of my childhood protests, from complaints about bad teachers to my desire for a later curfew. At the time, I thought he was just being a pessimist or giving me the brush-off, but in later years I came to realize that this adage was actually his way of challenging me to solve a problem myself, or to figure out a way around it.

The true test for us came in 1967, when my brother, serving as a marine in Vietnam, was wounded behind enemy lines. For weeks, we didn't know what had happened to Robert—if he had been captured or killed. Rather than succumb to grief, my father sprang to action and contacted our congressman for help. Finally, to our great relief Robert was located on a hospital ship—alive. It certainly "wasn't fair" that my family had been put through such a traumatic experience, or that my brother would have to spend what should have been his carefree college years in a naval hospital recovering from serious wounds. However, I never heard either my brother or my father complain or feel sorry for themselves; they just got on with life.

Indeed, life isn't fair. But somehow we always think it should be and are deeply disappointed when things don't pan out as hoped. What my father was trying to teach me was that, despite this obvious fault in the universe, it cannot be used as an excuse for not trying to be your best self. Instead, use unfairness as a starting point to be sure that your actions are the best you can muster, and find peace in navigating your time here with grace and humor whenever possible.

PART 4

BE UNREASONABLE

On Passion and Dreams

One person with passion is better than forty people merely interested.
— E. M. FORSTER

Loving what you do is like winning the lottery. It means that on most mornings getting up and getting going is relatively easy. (Okay, maybe not *every* morning.) It means that you aren't leading Thoreau's life of quiet desperation, or trapped in an Edward Hopper painting, going through the motions in a sepia-toned fog, feeling isolated and despondent.

Sometimes it takes a few tries to find your passion. At one time, I thought a career in advertising would be a perfect fit for me— glamorous and creative, like an updated version of *Mad Men*.

So during my senior year at the University of Virginia I came to New York to interview with several agencies. It was a cold, rainy March day and the wind turned my umbrella inside out. I couldn't find a cab, had a terrible cold, and my mascara was dripping down my face. Interviewer after interviewer looked at me patiently and either told me there was nothing available or to consider going to business school. Finally, after the head of personnel for Grey Advertising said, in essence, "Don't call us, we'll call you," I really impressed her. I started to cry. She suggested that I find a job closer to my parents . So much for my advertising career. Luckily the TV news thing worked out a bit better.

I love my job, and still marvel at my good fortune. I've been given amazing assignments and reported from some extraordinary places: the beaches of Normandy, the hills of Barcelona, the plains of Zimbabwe. I've witnessed, firsthand, unimaginable suffering in places like Haiti after the earthquake and war-torn Iraq and Afghanistan. I've gone down a bobsled run at close to a hundred miles per hour, been given a tour of the Reagan Library by Nancy Reagan herself. I've visited Number 10 Downing Street with Tony Blair and later Gordon Brown. I've flown to Petra in a helicopter piloted by the king of Jordan—a helicopter given to him by the sultan of Brunei. "Hey, it's good to be king."

There are also stories that serve as a constant reminder of the enormous responsibility that comes with this job. For me, and for many reporters, covering September 11 was the most challenging assignment of my career. As a single mother, I was worried about my girls. During a commercial break, I called my parents, who live not far from the Pentagon, and told them to go down to the basement. My heart broke every time I talked to someone who was desperately searching for a fiancé, a sister, a father. That story—that day—will be seared into my memory forever.

I've covered many history-making events on hot-button issues involving race, gender, and religion: the O.J. Simpson trial; the Rodney King verdict; the Anita Hill hearings; the brutal murder of Matthew Shepard, a young gay man in Wyoming; the controversy over building an Islamic center near Ground Zero. Doing my best to shed light on these critically important but often polarizing stories is incredibly challenging work, but I wouldn't have it any other way.

You may have some false starts, just like my foray into the ad world, but when you find a job you love, you can't imagine doing anything else. Of course, not everyone has the luxury of a career of choice, especially when the economy is lousy and jobs are hard to come by. But finding your passion will eventually get you to where you're supposed to be. And by the way, don't let money be your mantra. Focusing only on financial success often leaves you with a big bank account and a barren soul. As Twitter's Biz Stone says, think about what is *really* valuable.

Biz Stone

Co-Founder of Twitter

Think About What Is Valuable

Think about what is valuable before thinking about what is profitable and know that there's compound interest in helping others—start early!

(That's exactly 140 characters including spaces and punctuation!)

"Dr. Phil" McGraw

Mental Health Professional, Bestselling Author, and Television Host

Get Excited About Your Life

Every now and then, someone who's going through a tough patch will say to me, "Dr. Phil, you spend a lot of time helping others, but I know that, like everyone else, you have had to struggle in life. How did *you* handle it? After all, you couldn't go see Dr. Phil!"

Of course these people are right: There have been many times when I felt so low that down looked up. At points during my childhood, my family was flat-out dirt poor. Once, when my dad lost his job, he and I worked a paper route, throwing newspapers over a fifty-two-mile-long stretch just to keep food on the table. I never knew what it meant to feel settled, in part because my dad moved our family every three years—from Tulsa to Denver to Oklahoma City, and then on to Kansas City. With each move, I had to start over as the new kid in school, wearing hand-me-down clothes and eating lunch out of a paper sack, if I was lucky. I'm not sure anyone other than my mother saw much potential in me. I was an unremarkable student and, though today it's hard to believe, I wasn't a big talker. I shied away from my fellow students, my teachers, and other adults. My one hobby was sneaking out for a joyride in the family's broken-down car—if I could get the old jalopy going. One day, after I got caught in some mischief, my dad said to me, "Son, you couldn't be any dumber if we cut your head off!" He was kidding, of course (I think!), but if he had known all that I was up to behind his back, he might have tried it.

My saving grace, and what kept me showing up for school every day, was that I had become a pretty fair athlete—or so I thought. But one afternoon I had a wake-up call when my junior-high football team, which

I thought was the toughest, most intimidating bunch of bad dudes around, played a little makeshift Salvation Army team. I was poor but my school wasn't; we had really good equipment, coaches, and facilities. The opposing team had nothing. The kid who lined up across from me was wearing loafers instead of cleats and rolled-up blue jeans for football pants. Well, you can guess what happened. They beat us like they were clapping for a barn dance. One kid hit me so hard that I swear my shoulder *still* hurts these days when it rains! It was a turning point in my life. Why, I wondered, do some people with no advantages become champions, while those with all the advantages in the world end up failing? After the game, I asked my father, "What in the world just happened?" He said, "Well, son, you just got your butt handed to you on a platter! Those kids wanted it more than you did. Those kids had the 'eye of the tiger.'" From that moment on, regardless of my circumstances, I knew I wanted to have that same focus and passion in my own life.

As time passed, I began asking other questions. I wanted to know how a person could live a life of real meaning and genuine passion instead of just going through the motions. How can someone truly lead a life he or she wants instead of a life someone else wants for him or her? And, I asked over and over again, what must we do to remain perpetually filled with hope and optimism and energy in a world that is sometimes brutally harsh? I ended up taking three hundred hours of college courses and earning my doctorate in clinical psychology in an effort to answer those questions. I didn't always get the answers right, and there were times when I really struggled. For example, I spent twelve years trapped in a career that made me miserable. I stayed in it because I had created a prosperous life for my family and I didn't want to rock the boat. Still, I felt like a fraud because, although I was making money, I had no passion. Translation: I sold out. I didn't wake up excited in the morning. I wasn't proud of who I was or what I was doing day to day.

I finally realized that I had to break out of that comfort zone where my life felt safe and go after fulfilling the purpose for my being on this earth. I had to look back and "grade my own paper," so to speak, so that I wouldn't do the same stupid things again and again. I set out to reengineer those parts of my life that were not "me," and to build upon those that did feel right. Soon, I had a life that was authentically mine.

There's a reason I so often say to the guests on my television show, "The difference between winners and losers is that winners do things losers just don't want to do." It's the simple, unvarnished truth. To break out of the routine of life, you have to do what it takes to focus on staying true to yourself and to your own dreams. Instead of ignoring those dreams and hoping you can get around to them later on, you have to be committed to developing an action plan, to creating a "life script" with measurable goals, and to building a core of supporters around you to keep you going in the right direction.

Through these words, I hope I can save you some of the years I wasted. Go find your passion and embrace it. When you do, you will spring out of bed in the morning and sleep fast at night because you *love* what you are doing. There are many kinds of currency in life, not just monetary. I promise you will never regret this work for a moment, because life is not a dress rehearsal. This is your life—your one shot. So get excited and I'll see you out there in life kicking up your heels and having some fun.

Alicia Keys

Grammy Award–Winning Artist, Musician, Entrepreneur, Actress, and Activist

———

The Question

Throughout my life, I've been blessed to receive a lot of great advice just when I needed it most. My grandmother always used to tell me, "Nothing before its time," which I didn't understand for a while because I was far too impatient. But I now see that when you accept the fact that things will happen in their own time it takes a lot of pressure off, freeing you to put in the necessary work and follow the path before you.

The latest piece of advice that I'm living by is this: When making a very important business decision, I ask myself, "Would you still do it if you'd never see a dime from it?" I know that may sound crazy—who in the business world doesn't base part of their decisions on the prospective riches that some action might bring in the future (preferably the near future)? But I find that if the answer to the Question is yes, you will be following the path of your most authentic self. It's one of the easiest ways to figure out if that small voice in your head persuading you is your true instinct or that "other thing," which doesn't necessarily have the best motives.

It's so easy to be diverted, to chase something or to make a decision based on a falsely imagined outcome. I was once approached by a wealthy businessman who offered me an opportunity to create a business together. To many it would have seemed ideal, but I asked myself the Question, and realized that my answer was no. Soon afterward, I learned that this particular businessman was involved in some dealings that I surely would never want to be a part of, and so I said a silent prayer, grateful to have trusted myself.

When you make a decision because you really love what you're doing, because you're really passionate about it, believe in it, and because you'd do it no matter what the outcome—that's when you become most successful. Passion makes it much easier to eliminate the confusion, the clutter, and, more important, the garbage in life.

I truly believe that you can go anywhere you dream of going in life if you put in the work and are true to your heart. And if you ever find yourself feeling hesitant or confused (as we all do at some point) just ask yourself the Question.

Barbara Walters

Emmy Award–Winning Journalist and Bestselling Author of *Audition*

———

Follow Your Bliss

In college, I had a well-known professor whose advice was: "Follow your bliss." Practical application: Decide what you really would love to do . . . would do even if you didn't get paid. (But get paid.) Get a job in that industry or business. Start at any level. Get there first in the morning. Leave last at night. Fetch the coffee. Follow your bliss . . . but don't sleep with your boss. You will succeed.

Ina Garten

Bestselling Cookbook Author and Television Host

If You Love Doing It, You'll Be Very Good at It

In 1978, I was working at the White House on nuclear-energy policy and thinking, There's got to be more to life than this! When I wasn't working, though, I was cooking for my friends, which is what I really love to do. I'd been married to my husband, Jeffrey, for about ten years and I had taught myself to cook by studying Craig Claiborne's *The New York Times Cookbook* and Julia Child's *Mastering the Art of French Cooking*. One day, I was in my office reading *The New York Times* and my eye caught the Business Opportunities section, which I'd never read before. And there it was—a specialty food store called Barefoot Contessa for sale in a place I'd never been, the Hamptons, on the East End of Long Island.

That night I went home and told Jeffrey that I really needed to do something besides writing nuclear-energy-policy papers. He said, "Think of what you'd like to do that would be fun. Don't worry about making money—if you love doing it, you'll be very good at it." What amazing advice! I said, "Funny you should mention it—I just saw an ad for a specialty food store for sale." My sweet husband said, "Let's go look at it!" And so we drove up to Long Island, looked at the store, and my heart told me this was it. I made an offer on the spot, and the next day the owner called and said, "Thank you very much. I accept your offer." Yikes! I'd bought a food store!

In the next few months I was overwhelmed with excitement and fear—what made me think I could run a business? But Jeffrey's advice—"If you love doing it, you'll be very good at it"—kept me going. Often I worked twenty hours a day, but it never felt like work. I loved running the store, and over the next twenty years I built it into a successful business.

Then I decided it was time to try something new. A friend told me that type-A people (I think she was talking about me!) think they can figure out what to do next *while* they're doing something, but it never happens. She suggested that I stop working and spend the next year figuring it out. How scary is that? One day I was baking a thousand baguettes and running a store with forty employees, and the next day I had nothing to do. I have to admit, it was the hardest year of my life. But I know for sure that the next part of my career would never have happened without it. And this has been the happiest time of my life.

After I'd been struggling with one idea after another for most of the year, Jeffrey said, "Stay in the game. You love the food business—try something else in it." Out of sheer desperation to have something to do, I wrote a cookbook proposal, thinking I could do that while I figured out what was next. I had always thought writing a cookbook would be a lonely venture in a room by myself. Instead, I found myself working with a team of wonderful people! I loved testing recipes and I loved working on the book with editors, photographers, food stylists, prop stylists, and book designers. Which brings me to the final advice that I've learned along the way: You can't figure out what you want to do from the sidelines. You need to jump into the pond and splash around to see what the water feels like. You might like that pond or it might lead to another pond, but you need to figure it out *in* the pond.

After my second cookbook, *Barefoot Contessa Parties!,* was published, the Food Network asked me to do a television show. I was *extremely* reluctant, but I knew that the only way to see if it was right for me was to film a pilot. I needed to splash around in *that* pond. That was eight years ago, and it's impossible to explain how much television has changed my life and my business. I love what I do every day, and I've had amazing advice along the way that has made all the difference.

Joyce Carol Oates

National Book Award–Winning Author, Poet, Playwright, and Professor

———

"Here Is Life . . ."

Writers may seek advice, and writers may give advice, but writers rarely take advice. Why?

Because writers are stubbornly independent. Writers are self-reliant, knowing that there is no one to really help them but themselves; writers hope to be "original," which means not following in the paths of others.

Henry David Thoreau, one of our great American philosopher-poets, said, famously, "I have lived some thirty years on this planet, and I have yet to hear the first syllable of valuable or even earnest advice from my seniors. They have told me nothing, and probably cannot tell me anything, to the purpose. Here is life, an experiment to a great extent untried by me; but it does not avail me that they have tried it."

If there are a few—a very few—things I might tell young writers, or young artists of any kind, they are:

Never be ashamed of your subject, or of your passion for your subject.
Don't be discouraged!
Don't be envious of others!
Read widely—what you want to read, and not what someone suggests that you should read.
Forget "should."
Create your art for your own time, not for posterity.
Create your art for your own generation and for those a little older, and younger, than you. These will constitute your posterity.

Don't expect to be treated justly by the world, though you might try to treat others justly.

Don't too quickly make your mind up: You hate something, you love something else.

Don't too quickly cut yourself off from possibilities of experience.

Don't give up. Which is to say, don't be discouraged!

Take all advice with the proverbial grain of salt.

Chris Evert

Tennis Legend and Winner of Eighteen Grand-Slam Titles

Get Off the Sidelines!

Growing up, my siblings and I benefited from my parents' emphasis on the importance of both sports and academics. My sister Jeanne and I played the pro tour after high school, and my three other siblings received tennis scholarships at top colleges. My father, a professional tennis coach, was extremely proud of all our achievements. I would often ask him why he got us involved in tennis in the first place. I expected his answer to be that tennis offered opportunities to travel the world, or that playing on the tour was a good way to earn a living or to achieve fame. Instead, he quipped that tennis was a good way of keeping us off the streets and out of trouble. In more reflective moments, he'd say that he wanted to encourage us to set goals for ourselves and to learn the feeling of achievement.

As I get older, my father gets smarter. After having three children of my own, I understand what he meant about the value of setting goals. Having a passion in life, like a sport, keeps you busy and prevents idle time that can lead to temptation and wrong choices. Following a passion is also a source of self-esteem. As my children have grown up, each and every accomplishment has made them feel good about themselves, and as their mother I could not be more proud.

Hugh Jackman

Tony Award–Winning Actor and Producer

———

Trust Your Gut

1. Write down five things you *love* to do. Next, write down five things that you're really good at. Then just try to match them up! Revisit your list once a year to make sure you're on the right track.
2. Resist the urge to write lists, especially if the list is "Pros and Cons." Just go with your gut.
3. As the doctor who delivered my son said to me moments after his birth, "Don't rock the baby."
4. Learn to trust the feeling of "not knowing." For most of us, most of the time, that is the truth.
5. Oh, and take it from me, the label is right: *Don't Drink the Paint!*

Marc Shaiman

Oscar-Nominated, Tony/Grammy/Emmy Award–Winning
Composer, Lyricist, and Arranger

———

Oh, Miss Midler . . .

When I was around fourteen or so, I was exposed to the gargantuan talents of Bette Midler and became quite obsessed. I cut school once to take the bus from New Jersey to New York City to see her in concert. As she sang (and for many months after that), I imagined myself running down the aisle saying, "Oh, Miss Midler, I know every note of every arrangement of every song on every album of yours. Please let me play for you." In this daydream, I then sat down at the piano and was—of course—fantastic. From her perch atop the piano, Bette would look out at the audience with a "Damn, he's good!" expression. Nice dream.

When I was sixteen, having recently received my high school equivalency diploma, I went into the city with a friend to see an Off Broadway show. Afterward, we ran into some friends standing in front of a little bar and we all decided to stop in. Lo and behold, it was a piano bar—so of course I sat right down and started playing.

The bartender, sweeping up the bar (like right out of an old movie), stopped and said to me, "Stay right there." He ran out the door and came back a minute later accompanied by five people. They were rehearsing an act next door and explained that they needed a funnier piano player. They asked if I could play "cheesy," and I said, "You mean like at a bar mitzvah?" I played in that style and got the job playing with the troupe, who called themselves Cocktails for Five. One of those five people was named Scott, and he became my partner (in all ways) and we are about to celebrate our thirty-second anniversary. But that's a whole other story.

Anyway, I would stay with the Cocktails for Five gang on the weekends to play for their act and, as fate would have it, one of Bette Midler's backup girls (who are called the Harlettes) lived across the hall. The Harlettes were looking to do an act on their own and, to make a long story short, because I knew all about the harmonies they'd want (from studying Bette Midler records and the records those albums led me to), because I lived across the hall, and mostly because I would work for free, I got the gig.

The Harlettes' solo act was a hit, and Bette invited the girls to go back out on the road to open her show. I was flown to Los Angeles to put together the girls' opening act. After rehearsal the first day, I sat at the back of the hall as Bette herself came in to start her own rehearsal. At some point, she asked her band (all strangers to her repertoire) to play a song from her third album, *Songs for the New Depression*. The band members were stymied. One of the Harlettes whispered something in Bette's ear and pointed to me in the audience. Bette yelled out, "Hey, can you play 'No Jestering'?"

And I actually got to walk up to the stage saying, "Oh, Miss Midler, I know every note of every arrangement of every song on every album of yours. Please let me play for you."

So what's my point? To be a success, cut school and play the piano in an empty piano bar in order to meet your future lover and, subsequently, your idol? Well, that might be hard to re-create, but I will tell you this: Do not ever be afraid to dream, to imagine yourself doing exactly what you want to do in life, because it happened to me!

Matt Goldman

Co-Founder of the Blue Man Group and the Blue School

I Don't Want to Be Reasonable

In the late eighties, Phil Stanton, Chris Wink, and I dreamed up a crazy idea for a show called the Blue Man Group. We took to the stage in New York in 1987, appearing as a trio with cobalt-blue skin and plain black clothes who had no ears, no hair, and did not speak. From the start, Blue Man was often misunderstood. All he wants to do is connect. He wants to connect with his fellow Blue Men onstage, with his audience, with everyone and everything around him. When an audience member comes into the theater and sees this strange being—bald and blue—for the first time, the natural reaction is to think he's someone strange or alien. But a third of the way through the performance the audience realizes, "I'm actually watching myself, someone very human." Blue is not a mask that we put on. It's about what has been taken off. Once you take away hairstyle, skin tone, ethnicity, gender, and fashion—all the things that get us through our daily lives—what you're left with is the thing that is essentially human in all of us. I think that is why Blue Man has endured over the years; it allows us to look at ourselves with fresh eyes.

The first time Chris, Phil, and I went bald and blue, and looked in the mirror and at one another, if at that very moment I had said out loud, "We're going to make a living at this," someone would have carted me off to a padded cell. If, the first time we went bald and blue, I'd thought, *I'm going to make a living at this and play ten thousand shows in New York City, and an additional twenty-five thousand shows on five continents (North America, South America, Europe, Asia, and New Jersey);* if I'd said we would collaborate with artists like Moby, Dave Matthews, and the Kodo drummers; if I'd said to myself, *Yeah, we're going to sell out*

Lincoln Center and perform at a football stadium in front of eighty-five thousand people; if we'd imagined we were going to be nominated for a Grammy Award and perform live at the Grammys, to a standing ovation at the Staples Center; if I'd told you that all three of us would meet our wives at the show; that we'd get audience members to donate a few bucks at a time, adding up to three million dollars, to help families with AIDS; if I'd told you that we would go to the nation's capital and lobby senators and congressmen to fund music and arts education in the public school system; if I'd predicted that we would start an elementary school and sit on a panel discussing creativity with two Nobel Prize laureates, a British knight, a psychologist, and the Dalai Lama himself—if we had said all that the first time we went bald and blue, they'd have thrown us into that padded cell and tossed away the key. But that *is* what happened. That's what happened even though a lot of people—smart people, good-willed people, even loved ones and relatives—said that we were crazy. "It's not reasonable. It's weird. People won't get it. It's too smart. It's too childish. It's too strange. There's not enough humor. There's too much humor. It's too long, it's too short." You get the picture—we heard all the reasons why it was not going to work. But guess what? It did work.

The lesson here, to me at least, is this: Don't listen to anyone's advice. At least, don't listen to the advice of people who tell you what you can't do. Instead, find some good advisers whom you respect and trust and care about and listen to them. Then integrate what they are telling you with your own thinking, and really listen to yourself, your own learning, your gut instinct.

I wanted to be crazy, and I advise you to be crazy. To be weird. To be unreasonable. That's my favorite one. People are always saying, "Oh, come on, be reasonable!" And I want to shout, "No! I don't want to be reasonable!" I want to be completely unreasonable. I want to change the world. I want to be creative. I want to change the world creatively. And I want other people to be unreasonable with me.

Phil Stanton

Co-Founder of the Blue Man Group and the Blue School

Inspiration Lives in Unexpected Places

Something important took place in my life at the age of eighteen. It seemed mundane and pedestrian back then—maybe even a complete waste of time—and I never thought it would have any relevance to my future life. But in fact this experience has proved to be not only relevant but essential to the path I've taken in life: my first job out of high school.

I was born in Texas and raised in Georgia. I grew up being a little bit of a tinkerer and a builder, and I got those traits from my dad. He was a minister and a self-taught architectural designer, so he built homes and churches with his own two hands. At the time, I didn't have the slightest inclination to pursue a life in the theater. Even though both my mom and my dad were musicians and singers, I considered myself kind of shy and had no desire to be onstage. After graduating from high school, I needed to find work for the summer and a friend of the family got me a job in a hardware store—not a Home Depot like you find on every corner these days but a store that sold tons of industrial materials. I developed this geeky fascination with gears and nuts and bolts, PVC pipes, stainless steel, and different kinds of metal. Eventually, that job ended and I forgot about it for ten or twelve years. I ended up at a liberal arts college, where I bounced around between several majors until I finally found my element: acting. A few years later I was living in New York, where I met Chris Wink on my very first job as a waiter, and we became friends immediately. I met Matt Goldman soon after. Years later, the three of us would go on to create the Blue Man Group, a multimedia theatrical production that mixes music and comedy. But when we were just starting out, as we were conceiving the character of the Blue Man, all that stuff from my job at the hardware store years before came rushing back to me. All that fascination with pipe and metal and building materials. Matt, Chris, and I constructed strange instruments and other kinds of mechanical things as set pieces, and after scores of performances, television appearances, and tours around the world—well, the rest is history. The point here is that you will find your element, you will find your intelligence, if you pay attention to each and every experience life has to offer. Something you find along the way—even by accident— just might have the power to change your world.

Thomas Friedman

Bestselling Author and Pulitzer Prize–Winning
Columnist for *The New York Times*

————

Be an Untouchable, Do What You Love

Do what you love. This is not sappy career advice but an absolute survival strategy, because, as I like to put it, the world is getting flat. What is flattening the world is our ability to automate more work with computers and software and to transmit that work anywhere in the world so that it can be done more efficiently or cheaply, thanks to the new global fiber-optic network. The flatter the world gets, the more essential it is that you do what you love, because all the boring, repetitive jobs are going to be automated or outsourced in a flat world. The good jobs that will remain are those that cannot be automated or outsourced; they are the jobs that demand or encourage some uniquely human creative flair, passion, and imagination. In other words, jobs that can be done only by people who love what they do.

You see, when the world gets flat everyone should want to be an untouchable. Untouchables in my lexicon are people whose jobs cannot be outsourced or automated; they cannot be shipped to India or done by a machine. So who are the untouchables? Well, first among them are people who are really special—Michael Jordan or Barbra Streisand. Their talents can never be automated or outsourced. Second are people who are really specialized—brain surgeons, designers, consultants, or artists. Third are people who are anchored and whose jobs have to be done in a specific location—from nurses to hairdressers and chefs. Lastly—and this is going to apply to many of us, people who are really adaptable—are people who can change with changing times and changing industries.

There is a much better chance that you will make yourself special, specialized, or adaptable—a much better chance that you will bring that something extra—if you do what you love and love what you do.

I learned that quite by accident by becoming a journalist. It all started when I was in the tenth grade. First, I took a journalism class from a legendary teacher at my high school named Hattie Steinberg, who had more influence on me than any adult apart from my parents. Under Hattie's inspiration, journalism just grabbed my imagination. Hattie was a single woman nearing sixty by the time I had her as a teacher. She was the polar opposite of cool. But she sure got us all excited about writing, and we hung around her classroom like it was the malt shop and she was the disc jockey Wolfman Jack. To this day, her tenth-grade journalism class in Room 313 is the only journalism class I have ever taken. The other thing that happened to me in tenth grade, though, was that my parents took me to Israel over the Christmas break. And from that moment on I was in love with the Middle East. One of the first articles I ever published in my Minnesota high school paper was in the tenth grade, in 1969. It was an interview with an Israeli general who had been a major figure in the 1967 war. He had come to give a lecture at the University of Minnesota; his name was Ariel Sharon. Little did I know how many times our paths would cross in the years to come.

Anyway, by the time tenth grade was over I still wasn't quite sure what career I wanted, but I knew what I loved: I loved journalism, and I loved the Middle East. Now, growing up in Minnesota at that time, in a middle-class household, I never thought about going away to college. Like all my friends, I enrolled at the University of Minnesota. But, unlike my friends, I decided to major in Arabic and Middle Eastern studies. There were not a lot of kids at the University of Minnesota studying Arabic back then. Norwegian, yes; Swedish, yes; Arabic, no. But I loved it. My parents didn't mind; they could see that I enjoyed it. But if I had a dime for every time one of my parents' friends said to me, "Say, Tom, your dad says you're studying Arabic—what are you going to do with that?" Well, frankly, it beat the heck out of me. But this was what I loved, and it just seemed that that was what college was for.

I eventually graduated from Brandeis with a degree in Mediter-ranean studies and went on to graduate school at Oxford. During my first year in England—this was 1975—I was walking down the street with my then girlfriend and now wife, Ann, and I noticed a front-page headline from the *Evening Standard*. It said, "President Carter to Jews: If Elected I Promise to Fire Dr. K." I thought, Isn't that interesting? Jimmy Carter is running against Gerald Ford for president, and in order to get elected he's trying to win Jewish votes by promising to fire the first-ever Jewish secretary of state. I thought about how odd that was and what might be behind it. And for some reason I went back to my dorm room in London and wrote a short essay about it. No one asked me to; I just did it. Well, my then girlfriend, now wife's family knew the editorial-page editor of the *Des Moines Register,* and my then girlfriend, now wife brought the article over to him when she was home for spring break. He liked it, printed it, and paid me fifty dollars for it. And I thought that was the coolest thing in the whole world. I was walking down the street, I had an idea, I wrote it down, and someone gave me fifty dollars. I've been hooked ever since. A journalist was born, and I never looked back.

So whatever you plan to do in life, don't just listen to your head. Listen to your heart. It's the best career counselor there is. Do what you really love to do, and if you don't know quite what that is yet, well, keep searching, because once you find it you'll bring that something extra to your work that will help ensure that you will not be automated or outsourced. It will make you untouchable.

Wynton Marsalis

Internationally Acclaimed Musician, Composer, Bandleader, and Educator

―――

Commit with Your Whole Heart

When I was a senior in high school, all my teachers and advisers said, "Don't major in music because it's too difficult to make a living. You need a 'real' profession to fall back on when the dream dies." Because I was a pretty good student, one teacher even said, "Why would you waste your brain on music?" My mother told me, "Child, if you go into music you're gonna end up struggling and suffering just like your daddy." When I talked to my father, a great musician whom I had seen killing himself to make barely enough to take care of his family, he said, "Make sure you don't have anything to fall back on . . . because you will. This is not for the faint of heart."

Vera Wang
Internationally Acclaimed Fashion Designer

Life by Design

My life and my career have always been about a singular need and passion for self-expression. Whether it was my love of figure skating or my devotion to fashion: either way, both obsessions allowed me to envision a world of my own through which I could continue to learn and grow, artistically and creatively. For young people everywhere, I have some words of advice that, hopefully, will encourage them to search for their dream, live it, and embrace it. So here we go . . .

First, most of us do not necessarily grow up knowing what we want to do; that is a fallacy. Life is a process, and most of the time it's impossible to predict where the journey will lead us. In my case, the journey to becoming a fashion designer started out on another path altogether. When I failed to qualify for the U.S. Olympic figure skating team, I realized that I had to find something that fascinated and captivated me as much as skating had. The dedication and determination necessary to compete at any élite level is so enormous, it is hard to replace that focus with just anything.

My subsequent trip to Paris, where I studied at the Sorbonne, was the very opportunity I needed to discover a whole new world apart from skating. I came home from the fashion capital of the world determined to chart my own career in fashion. That began with *Vogue* magazine, where I worked for seventeen years, followed by a stint as a design director at Ralph Lauren. Ultimately, my journey led to the creation of my own fashion company, twenty years later.

We are all frightened by change and by the unfamiliar, but those who remain open—despite their hesitations—can discover new worlds and opportunities. I'm always asked by budding fashionistas out there, "How do you get into fashion?" The best advice I can give is to study it, as you would acting or figure skating. School is a great place to start, but if that's not accessible to you then try learning it from the ground up: Xeroxing, folding stock in a store, selling—at least, by experiencing it firsthand, you'll find out if you really love it. If you already know your path and are fortunate enough to know yourself, the next best thing is to work for a designer, publicist, or publication that you truly admire. That way, you can learn how multifaceted the fashion world really is and how each business has its own specific DNA and business model.

Last, regardless of your passion, most people only begin to truly appreciate their careers, and their lives, as they improve and grow and achieve their goals on their own! That is where true satisfaction and dignity lie for all of us. No one can ever take something away from you if you've earned it. That is the beauty of achievement!

PART 5

MINUTE PARTICULARS

On Doing What's Right

Good manners sometimes means simply putting up with other people's bad manners. —H. Jackson Brown, Jr.

The English poet William Blake once observed, "He who would do good to another man must do it in Minute Particulars." Minute particulars. Not grand gestures but everyday acts of kindness. They accumulate, and together provide the threads that make up our moral fiber. The writer Annie Dillard put it another way: "How we live our days, of course, is how we live our lives." I listened to my minister, the Reverend Michael Lindvall, talk about "minute particulars" one Sunday and was struck by how closely his sermon aligned with my personal philosophy—or, at least, with the kind of person I strive to be.

Anyone who has taken Psych 101 is familiar with a concept called modeling. Good manners beget good manners, along with endless appeals to "put your napkin in your lap!" My dad was obsessed with a firm handshake and eye contact, as am I. My daughters could win gold medals for both. Kindness also begets kindness. It always gives me great pleasure and pride when I see my children showing people the respect they deserve—when they thank someone politely and tell him or her to have a good day, or hold the door for an elderly shopper. These are common courtesies that sometimes seem woefully uncommon. Parents have so much responsibility when it comes to shaping young minds—and an obligation to teach compassion, empathy, and tolerance, primarily through example.

I am a sucker for musicals. I know the words to almost every song written by Rodgers and Hammerstein. In fact, if I could have a career in anything besides TV, and if I had the God-given talent, I would be a Broadway-musical star. When I auditioned for my high school musical *Carnival,* I had fantasies of getting the lead role of Lily. Unfortunately, that went to Laurie Kittler. I was cast as a deaf person who didn't speak. But I digress. I recently saw a revival of one of my very favorite musicals, *South Pacific,* at Lincoln Center. I was struck by the prescient lyrics sung by Lieutenant Cable:

> You've got to be taught to be afraid
> Of people whose eyes are oddly made,
> And people whose skin is a different shade,
> You've got to be carefully taught.

You've got to be taught to be accepting and kind and open-minded. You've got to be taught to stand up for the kid who's getting bullied. You've got to be taught to speak out and take a stand against all kinds of bad behavior.

Being a good person pays off. If you're kind and generous to your co-workers, they'll celebrate your success. It will also keep your head from getting too big. When I was promoted to co-anchor of the *Today* show, a crusty older producer who'd seen it all told me something I'll never forget. "Kid," he said, holding his cigarette languidly, "today you may be drinking the wine. Tomorrow you could be picking the grapes." In other words, don't get too big for your britches, kid. All those people you pass as you climb the ladder of success could be the same ones who will catch you if you fall.

The digital landscape often sends us a different message. It's so easy—and cowardly—to be an anonymous hater. Don't let civil discourse become an oxymoron. Elevate the conversation online and in life. Rejecting nastiness that's pervasive is brave and bold. The Internet is a miraculous, powerful, and equalizing tool. We've seen it expose repressive regimes and spur uprisings that can change the face of a nation. But it can also be a cesspool of snarkiness. Don't get sucked in. In his book *Snark,* David Denby writes, "Snark often functions as an enforcer of mediocrity and conformity. In its cozy knowingness, snark flatters you by assuming that you get the contemptuous joke. You've been admitted, or readmitted, to a club, though it may be the club of the second-rate."

Old-fashioned qualities like integrity, honor, and character may sound corny, but no matter how old you are they are qualities that never go out of style. As you'll soon see—just ask Momo!

Bob Schieffer

Emmy Award–Winning Journalist, Chief Washington Correspondent
of CBS News, and Anchor of *Face the Nation*

Momo's Rules

My mother was a child of the Depression who was widowed at the age of forty-five, with three children. She devoted herself to us and was the driving force in our lives.

Like many grandparents, she was named by her grandchildren; but before she became Momo she raised us by a simple set of rules that I still live by—and, in truth, still live in fear of violating. She was one formidable woman.

Momo's rules, in no particular order:

1. Never lie, cheat, or steal.

No explanation required, but heaven help the one of us who violated that rule—and she set her expectations high. Once, my brother's friends were jailed for a college prank and my brother, who had innocently stayed out of trouble, thought that he deserved some credit. "Credit for what?" Momo replied. "I didn't send you to college to get thrown in jail. That's the least I expect of you."

2. It is better to get to the airport too early than too late.

To Momo, punctuality was next to godliness. Maybe that's why I never missed a flight or a deadline in more than fifty years as a reporter. To this day, I still think of her every time I go to an airport.

3. **When you are doing something important, make sure you have a smile on your face and a shine on your shoes.**

Throughout my life, I have never applied for a job, gone on an important assignment, or shown up for an interview without first checking my shoes, which always makes me think of Momo and smile. Did freshly shined shoes lead to some of my better interviews? Probably not. But she believed that a man who didn't care about his personal appearance showed a lack of respect for himself. "If you don't respect yourself, why should anyone else respect you?" she asked.

4. **Go vote! It makes you feel big and strong.**

I can't remember a time in my life when politics didn't dominate the conversation at our house. My mother loved politics and always said, "If you don't vote, you can't complain about what you get." To this day, I take the same delight that she did in voting for those I like (and sometimes greater pleasure in voting against those I don't like). And I always vote, because I know that if I don't she'll come back and give me a good going-over.

I wouldn't wish Momo's punishments for violating her rules on anyone, but her methods worked well for our family. Not a day passes that I don't think of Momo and what she taught us. From what I can tell, my daughters are raising their own children by the same rules. Momo would have liked that. Actually, she would have expected it.

General Ray Odierno
United States Commander in Iraq

—

Real Success

I agree with William Arthur Ward that "greatness is not found in possessions, power, position, or prestige. It is discovered in goodness, humility, service, and character."

Rania Al Abdullah
Queen of Jordan

—

Through Other Eyes

Thirteen years ago, I was having a casual breakfast with my beloved father-in-law, the late King Hussein, when he looked me straight in the eye and asked me a simple question: "What do you think of me?"

Here was a man whose very name was synonymous with strength, courage, and determination. The only thought to cross my mind was "How can a world leader of *your* stature possibly care about *my* opinion?"

Later, I understood why King Hussein had asked me that question: He wanted to see himself through someone else's eyes. Only later did I realize that he had been asking that question of people all his life. It wasn't about flattery or insecurity. It wasn't about pride or arrogance. It was about humility—the greatest virtue of any leader.

As human beings, we are all works in progress, and none of us is above a little self-reflection. If we see ourselves as others see us, we begin to appreciate our kaleidoscopic dimensions. If we value one another's perspectives, we add more depth to our own. And if we concede our imperfections, we grant ourselves space to improve.

That's how we serve those around us more fully and lovingly. That's how we give of ourselves more wholly. That's how King Hussein did it: The more open he became, the more he found he could contain.

It was quite a breakfast.

Jay Leno

Comedian and Host of *The Tonight Show*

Be Open to Other People

I had very good parents. My mother came to this country from Scotland by herself when she was eleven, and she didn't have much of an education. My dad was kind of a street kid, and he eventually went into the insurance business selling nickel policies door-to-door. It was the 1930s, a time when America was a lot more racist and segregated than it is now. One day my dad asked his boss, "What's the toughest market to sell?" and the insurance guy replied, "Well, black people. They don't buy insurance." My dad thought, But they have kids, they have families. Why wouldn't they buy insurance? So he said, "Give me Harlem." He took the Harlem territory and sold nickel policies; every Friday he would go around and collect the nickel and give his customers a receipt on the policy.

When my dad died in 1994, I talked about him on *The Tonight Show*. I told the story of how he worked in Harlem and how he always taught us to be open-minded and not to say or think racist things. Then one day I got a letter from a woman who was about seventy-five years old. She wrote that when she was a little girl a man used to come to her house to collect policies and he would always bring her a lollipop. She said this man was the only white person who had ever come to dinner at their house, and the only white person she had ever had dinner with period until she got to be almost an adult. This man was very kind to her, she said, and his name was Angelo—was this my father? The letter really made me cry. I called her up and said that, yes, that was in fact my dad, and she told me how kind he was to her family. Her whole attitude toward white people was based on that one nice man she met in her childhood, who always treated her with kindness and respect, and always gave her a piece of candy and asked her what she wanted to be when she grew up. From this experience, I learned a valuable life lesson never to judge people, and to be open-minded and kind to others.

Gloria Steinem
Writer and Feminist Organizer

Top Ten Pieces of Advice I Just Made Up
for Myself—See If Any Help You

1. If it looks like a duck and walks like a duck and quacks like a duck but you think it's a pig, it's a pig.

2. Marx was smart about a lot of things, but not about the end justifying the means. Actually, the means dictate the ends. We won't have laughter and kindness and poetry and pleasure at the end of any revolution unless we have laughter and kindness and poetry and pleasure along the way.

3. Laughter is the most revolutionary emotion, because it's free and can't be forced. Fear can be compelled. Even love can be compelled if we're kept isolated and dependent long enough. But laughter comes from an "Aha!" place of sudden understanding when known things come together and make something new. Einstein had to be careful while shaving because when he suddenly had an "Aha!" he laughed and cut himself.

4. There's more variation *among* human groups than *between* human groups. "Masculine" and "feminine" are created roles, as are ideas of race and class. So when making any generalized statement about women and men, substitute, say, "Gentiles and Jews," "whites and blacks," or "rich and poor." If it's still acceptable, okay. If it's not, it's not.

5. For ninety-five percent of human history, spirituality placed god in all living things. Then god was withdrawn from women and nature to make it okay to conquer women and nature. As a smart Egyptologist said, "Monotheism is but imperialism in religion." Here's the good news: What humans did, humans can undo.

6. Religion is too often politics in the sky. When God looks like the ruling class, we're in deep shit. When there's a limited priesthood, it's deeper. When we're told to obey in order to get a reward after death, it's deepest. Now that doomsday religions have coincided with doomsday weapons, it may mean life or death to return spirituality to religion.

7. The Golden Rule was written by smart folks for people who were superior: *Treat others as you would want to be treated.* Especially women, but also men who've been inferior, need to reverse this: *Treat yourself as well as you treat others.*

8. Labeling makes the invisible visible, but it's limiting. Categories are the enemy of connecting. *Link, don't rank.*

9. All five of our senses exist *only* in the present. We can't fully live in the past or the future—or even in Computer Land. *Right now, where you are is all there is.*

10. If even one generation was born without ranking and raised without violence, we have no idea what might be possible on this Spaceship Earth.

Madeleine K. Albright

Sixty-fourth Secretary of State of the United States,
Chair of Albright Stonebridge Group

Never Play Hide-and-Seek with the Truth

I was born in Prague shortly before Germany invaded in what proved to be the opening act of World War II. My parents and I escaped to England and spent the war there. My father worked for the Czechoslovak government-in-exile while I attended a series of schools, including, at age six, the Ingomar School in Walton-on-Thames. My report cards were generally favorable but also indicated that I "took a little while to settle down" and needed to work harder to "avoid careless slips." These admonishments reflected my state of mind. As a Czechoslovak girl in a foreign land and the eldest child of busy parents, I was full of energy and the desire to please.

During recreation periods at school, the entire student body divided into Harry Potter–like teams that earned points for various activities. When I first scored points for my team, I reported the accomplishment to my father, who praised me. Eager to elicit more signs of approval, I began to recount exploits for which I was supposedly awarded additional points; these heroics included, as I recall, pulling my teacher out of a rosebush. Pretty soon I had racked up such a high score that I decided to invent a special award. That evening I burst through the front door of my house saying that I had won the Egyptian Cup. My beaming parents asked me to bring the trophy home, which obviously I could not do. In desperation, I thought up a whole series of new lies to tell about how awful everyone was being to me. "They even make me sit on needles!" I exclaimed. My ever-protective mother insisted on rushing to school to find out what injustices were being inflicted upon her poor child. The appalling truth came out, and I was punished with appropriate severity.

In later years, whenever a story I was telling seemed at odds with the truth my parents had only to say, "Egyptian Cup," and I stopped.

The moral of the story is: Never play hide-and-seek with the truth, because those who try too hard to build themselves up will have no one else to blame when they come tumbling down.

Nia Vardalos

Academy Award–Nominated Writer and Actress

Be Polite

I don't like conflict.

I'm a middle child and I'm Canadian.

So, to me, rudeness is a foreign language.

I've been very fortunate to work with wonderful actors, producers, directors, and crews. *My Big Fat Greek Wedding* was my first film experience, and the producers treated me like gold before that movie made a dime. Perhaps that's why I continue to make movies with them. Or maybe it's simply because they're polite. They have good manners.

I think good manners come from good parents.

I'm a parent now, and of course I want to be good at it, so one day I went to my daughter's kindergarten class to observe. I was surprised to see that she and her classmates had already figured out that a temper tantrum doesn't resolve anything.

Sometimes, on movie sets, people act like babies. I just want to pass out the diapers and pacifiers when a director yells at the crew, or producers shriek at underpaid assistants. I've heard cinematographers make snide remarks about actresses' looks. And the thespian hissy fit makes me wonder if maybe someone was weaned off the breast a tad too soon.

The reason for this rude behavior is simply this: Making movies is a lot of pressure. And some people aren't able to handle it. In tense circumstances, people act out. They forget their manners.

For me, filming a movie is like hosting a party. I like to see that everyone has a drink and a snack, is mingling, smiling, and then . . . let's act.

Sure, I've seen conflict. Being passive on a film set is not the norm. Filmmakers are opinionated, passionate people. Disagreement, even loud, vehement arguing is fine, even healthy, and it usually leads to a better solution and a more original film. But that's not what I mean here. I'm talking about the adult tantrum. I mean . . . that one strange person who's not fun to be around.

The truth of the matter is, every time you start a new job, in any field, everyone sizes each other up. People wait to see who's the chatty one, who's the needy one, who's high-maintenance, who's moody. And usually one person will reveal him- or herself to be the Problem. That person is usually the one who can't handle the pressure and who wasn't given—or didn't heed—the parental guidance on how to resolve conflict. And, inevitably, disputes do come up in most work environments. It's how you deal with conflict that matters.

There are people who just need chaos. Perhaps it's a way of trying to achieve power, or maybe it's just emotional immaturity. Maybe it's a deep psychological desire to re-create the environment they were raised in. Whatever the reason, some people need to be surrounded by angst. And these people get annoyed when they can't create drama. It's almost as if they want to pull others into that pit of bad behavior.

So my advice is this: Don't let them.

I suggest that, when encountering rudeness, you respond with politeness. Take the high road and invite that person to join you. If he or she persists—well, then the game is on.

I'll let you in on a little secret here. We middle-child Canadians are nice. But we're not idiots. So the ruder people get, the nicer I become.

It drives them nuts.

If someone yells, just laugh at the fun, loud noise the person's making. If he or she makes sarcastic comments, act as if you don't get it. The more the person boils, just break into song, hug other co-workers, treat everyone to pizza and drinks. Simply refuse to let the energy vampire suck the life out of the room.

In most work environments, there will be that one person. In fact, if you can't spot the problem person everyone's talking about, it might be you.

And, yes, when you're that person people do talk about you. People do make fun of you. And they do have a nickname for you that rhymes with basshole.

But mostly we just shake our heads and wonder what kind of parents you had.

So be polite.

Even if people are being rude to you.

In that case, be extra polite.

Because, let's be honest . . . it is sort of satisfying to watch them implode.

Suze Orman
Internationally Acclaimed Personal-Finance Expert

___

Do What Is Right, Not What Is Easy

Something a lot of people don't know about me is that I was a waitress until I was about thirty years old, and I really had no plans to be anything other than a waitress. After four years of working my way through school at the University of Illinois—I didn't even graduate until a few years later—I got into my Ford Econoline van, which my brother Bobby helped me buy for fifteen hundred dollars, and headed out west to California with three friends. I'd never been anywhere or seen anything in my life, and I was going for it. When we got to California, I lived on the streets of Berkeley for three months in the van because I had no money to my name. Then I landed my dream job as a waitress at the Buttercup Bakery. This was 1973 and I was twenty-two years old. I worked as a waitress at the Buttercup Bakery for seven years, making four hundred dollars a month. In 1980, I decided that I wanted to be more than a waitress. I wanted to own my own restaurant, so I called my mom and dad and asked for twenty thousand dollars to open up my own place. My mom said, "Suze, honey, that's more money than we have to our name," and I said, "Mom, I'm so sorry, I don't know what I was thinking."

I went to work the next morning feeling depressed. A customer named Fred Hasbrook, whom I'd been waiting on for many years, came in—I made him a Jack-cheese-and-ham omelet every morning for seven years—and he said, "What's wrong, Sunshine? You don't look happy." I told Fred the story about how I wished I could open up my own restaurant and how it wasn't going to happen. Fred sat back down with the other gentlemen I'd been waiting on, a group that met every morning at seven o'clock to eat breakfast before work, and told them my story. Before he left, Fred came up and handed me personal checks and commitments on little scraps of paper totaling fifty thousand dollars, with a note written on a little napkin that said:

> This is for people like you, so that your dreams can come true. To be paid back in ten years, if you can, with no interest.

I looked at him in disbelief and said, "Fred, I have two questions: Are these checks going to bounce like all of mine do?" He laughed, and then I said, "Fred, I have no idea what to do with this money. Where do I even put it?" It was more money than I had ever seen in my life! Fred said to me, "Go down to your local Merrill Lynch office and put it in a money-market account for now until I can help you." And I said, "I have another question for you. What's a Merrill Lynch money-market account?" I had never heard of such a thing. Fred told me what I needed to know, and the next day I went to the Oakland office of Merrill Lynch intending to put my cash into a money market, paying eighteen percent interest.

When I walked in, I was given to what's called the "broker of the day," the one financial adviser who gets every new person walking in the door, and his name was Randy. Well, I walked in and Randy sat me down and I told him that this money was going to help me open up my new restaurant. He looked at me and asked, "While it's sitting there, how would you like to make a hundred dollars a week on it?" I said, "Are you kidding? That's what I make in a whole week as a waitress," and he told me to sign on the dotted line. I signed the papers. They were blank, and I didn't even think about it. Here was this impressive guy in a pin-striped suit, and I just went along and said, "Okay."

What I found out later is that the papers Randy had me sign were called option agreements, which if correctly filled out and signed allow you to invest in one of the most speculative strategies of all: buying options. At that time nearly ninety percent of all people who bought only options lost their money; they are very high-commission, very fast, and very speculative. But to be able to qualify to invest in options you have to have the money to do so. Randy had filled out the paperwork as if I were a very sophisticated investor, and Merrill Lynch had given its stamp of approval, so Randy was able to take my fifty thousand dollars and invest it in options. Well, the first week or two I made five thousand dollars, and I thought I'd died and gone to heaven. I couldn't believe my luck. Very shortly after that, I lost the entire fifty thousand.

Now I didn't know what to do. I kept remembering my father at this moment in time; he never gave up, no matter what. So I picked myself up and I thought, Hey, if people like Randy can be a broker, I can be a broker, too—after all, they just make you broker! I got dressed in my red-and-white striped Sassoon pants, tucked into my white cowboy boots, with a blue silk shirt on top—it was the only fancy outfit I had (or what I thought was fancy)—and I walked into Merrill Lynch to apply for a job. Nobody knew what to do with me. They'd never had a woman stockbroker before in the Oakland office.

I wound up sitting in the manager's office, and he said to me, "Listen, I personally believe women belong barefoot and pregnant. But I'm going to hire you." He never said it outright, but I assume he had to hire me in order to fulfill the women's quota, because right after that he also said, "But you will be out of here in six months—trust me on that one." So I looked at him and said, "How much are you going to pay me to get me pregnant?" And he answered, "Fifteen hundred dollars a month." I said, "I'll take it." As I left the office, his secretary, Lori, gave me a book on how to dress for success. I was in shock at landing the job and I had no clothes whatsoever, so I went down to Macy's in San Francisco. The store gave me a credit card with a three-thousand-dollar limit after verifying that I did, in fact, have a job with Merrill Lynch for fifteen hundred dollars a month. I bought my new clothes and was ready to go.

I went to work every single day at Merrill Lynch scared to death because I felt like I didn't belong there. I was driving a 1967 Volvo station wagon while everybody else drove a brand-new Mercedes or a BMW. They all parked in the parking lot, but I parked in the street and risked getting tickets (knowing I could go to court and pay off the fines with community service) because I didn't have money for the lot. I ate lunch by myself at Taco Bell for two years straight, while all the other brokers went out to fancy places. They invited female strippers in for the men's birthday parties, and I guess they expected me to be fine with it, or else they didn't really care. I had never hidden the fact that I was gay, so maybe they thought I would enjoy the performance as well.

A few months into the job, while I was studying for my Series 7 exam, a test that all brokers have to pass, I realized that what Randy had done with my fifty thousand dollars was illegal. There is a rule that a stockbroker cannot invest a client's money in a way that is inappropriate for that client. Randy knew that I couldn't afford to lose my money, and that I had plans to open a business, so my money should have been kept in the money-market fund. I got up all my courage and marched into the manager's office and told him that he had a crook working for him. The manager told me, "Suze, that crook makes us a lot of money. You need to go sit down in your little cubicle and say nothing." And I said, "Yes, sir."

I sat down at my desk and thought to myself, *Oh my God. I'm young, I'm only thirty years old. Fred told me I didn't have to pay back the loan unless I could, and at no interest, so I could just sit here and do nothing. But what if it wasn't me, what if it was my mother, or grandmother, or somebody who didn't have time to recover?* I would look over at Randy and see older people in his office, and imagine that he was doing the same thing to them that he had done to me. This was the turning point in my life, because at that moment I had to decide if I was going to do what was right or what was easy. It was easy to sit there and do absolutely nothing, but it wasn't right. So I did the only thing that I could think to do: I found the name of a lawyer who took on securities cases. I went to see him and told him my story. He accepted the case on a contingency basis, and we ended up suing Merrill Lynch.

Now, what I didn't know at the time was that because I had sued Merrill Lynch, I couldn't be fired. During the two years that the case was under investigation, I became one of the top-producing brokers in the Oakland office, and it was all by doing what was right for people. Eventually, the manager who had originally given me six months on the job was moved to another position, and a new manager came in who settled the suit immediately because he saw that it was wrong. Randy had been let go shortly after I brought the suit. Merrill Lynch paid me back all of my money plus interest, which allowed me to pay back Fred Hasbrook and my friends from the Buttercup Bakery. And the rest is history.

Through it all, two of the greatest lessons of my life emerged: First, you must always do what is right, not what is easy. And second, every no leads you that much closer to a yes. Every loss leads to a gain. I would not be the person I am today if I had not lost it all, kept the belief in myself, and done what was right rather than what was easy by always putting people first, before money.

Beyoncé

Grammy Award–Winning Singer, Songwriter, Performer, Actress, and Designer

———

Take Time to Know Yourself

Knowing who you are is the greatest wisdom a human being can possess. Know your goals, what you love, your morals, your needs, your standards, what you will not tolerate and what you are willing to die for. It defines who you are. I have learned not to obsess over being number one all the time. Sometimes not being number one gives you the incentive and the courage to fight harder; it is motivating. Have patience. Have grace. Be secure enough in yourself to base success on personal growth.

Take at least twenty minutes every day to be still and quiet. Time to sit in complete silence. Think. Reflect. Dissect your thoughts and feelings. Relive any mistakes from the day before. Decide how to be smarter and tougher, how to be more committed and considerate of others and more sensitive and aware of your surroundings. Choose something you learned that will make you a better person.

Choose to be happy and positive. Live like the blessed human you are. Define you. Knowing who you are allows you to create your own beautiful legacy.

Mehmet Oz, M.D.

Surgeon, Television Host, and Bestselling Author

Take Time to Really Listen

In my final year of surgical training, I was called to see a petite fifty-three-year-old Jehovah's Witness with an aggressive bleeding stomach ulcer. In keeping with their religious beliefs, Jehovah's Witnesses refuse to receive blood transfusions. The problem facing my patient was that her hematocrit—the percentage of red blood in her body—was at only seventeen percent. The normal value is forty-five percent, and in this precarious setting it was standard procedure to transfuse blood in order to keep the figure above thirty percent. She needed surgery, and I needed the safety net of blood in her veins to afford me time to complete the operation. I approached my fading patient and her family. To my dismay, they were firmly opposed to a blood transfusion.

My only hope was emergency surgery—a desperate attempt to stop the bleeding in time. We were in the operating theater within minutes, but I already knew that we were too late. By the time the bleeding ulcer was sewn closed, the hematocrit was down to four percent. By way of comparison, healthy baboons die at blood counts of seven percent, and this frail woman had just undergone major surgery. She didn't stand a chance.

The surgical team felt distraught and powerless. I was angry that the stubborn, medically illogical beliefs of this family were preventing me from saving a life. I stormed through the hallway toward the large family that waited outside the Intensive Care Unit. Exasperated, I explained what had occurred in the OR and stressed that the patient's life would most definitely be lost if we could not transfuse her. Too little blood remained to provide her fifty-three-year-old heart with the oxygen needed to survive. Already the electrical ECG strip showed that the heart was dying. The decision-makers of the family needed to determine whether they were willing to sacrifice the life of their matriarch upon the altar of their religion. I left and gave them five minutes to decide.

I returned to an eerily calm waiting room. An older gentleman came forward and briefly explained that their God would protect her and that they would rather see their loved one die than go against the tenets of their religion. I was livid. I felt that, in standing on principle, the family had abandoned their matriarch. They knew nothing of what was happening to her medically, yet they were condemning her to death. I left the ICU banging my stethoscope against my thigh in disgust. I refused to be present when she died from a very preventable ailment: the lack of blood.

The matriarch survived the first evening, and the next, and another, until she was released from the hospital eleven days later with a hematocrit of nine. Though her levels were still low, the ruby color of her cheeks had returned and she was well enough to go home.

We doctors are taught early in our training that if we really listen to our patients, deep insights will shine through for us. I realized that I had been angry at my patient's family because of my perception that they were disbelieving my advice. I was wrong. They absolutely trusted my judgment and predictions, yet firmly believed that their mother was better off in heaven without blood than alive on earth having sacrificed her religious principles.

Many times in my career I have cared for thoughtful souls who understood that, even though their decisions went against my medical advice, they were still making the right decisions for their own lives. Even though I still disagree with the choice made by my Jehovah's Witness patient, the experience taught me to listen more acutely to what my patients—as well as my friends and family—are really trying to say and to stop judging their comments as a referendum on me. Knowledge offers a wonderful perspective, but the wisdom to correctly guide our life decisions is deeply ingrained in each of us if we take the time to listen.

Kevin, Joe, and Nick Jonas

The Jonas Brothers, Recording Artists, Musicians, and Actors

———

Remember Where You Come From

Our grandfather Paul Adam Jonas gave our father a piece of advice when he left for college, and this advice has been passed down to us through the generations. As Grandpa Jonas said, "Live like you are at the bottom, even if you are at the top." For us, this has been a nudge on a daily basis to remember where we come from, and to live with humility and gratitude in our actions no matter where life takes us.

Sheryl Crow

Grammy Award–Winning Singer-Songwriter

Do the Best You Can

I have learned all my best lessons by diligently attending the school of hard knocks. Somewhere along the way, my mother and trusty adviser turned me on to a book called *The Four Agreements,* by Don Miguel Ruiz.

The book is thin and a very quick read, with the four agreements being: (1) Don't take things personally. (2) Don't make assumptions. (3) Make your word impeccable. (4) Do the best you can. Those four simple tenets are reminders to me, on a daily, moment-to-moment basis, how I can have a more easygoing and enjoyable life. I often fall short of perfection, and I will take personally something that has nothing to do with me or catch myself joining in idle gossip. I have even been known to make the odd assumption about what others ought to be doing. But under the umbrella of the "Do the best you can" rule falls all the challenges one can accept for being the best person one can be in all she does.

Thomas Friedman

Bestselling Author and Pulitzer Prize–Winning
Columnist for *The New York Times*

———

Be a Skeptic, Not a Cynic

Always remember, there is a difference between skepticism and cynicism. Too many journalists, and too many of our politicians, have lost sight of that boundary line. I learned that lesson very early in my career. In 1982, while working in the Business section of the *Times,* I was befriended by a young editor named Nathaniel Nash. Nathaniel was a gentle soul and a born-again Christian. He liked to come by and talk to me about Israel and the Holy Land. In April 1982, the *Times* assigned me to cover the Lebanese civil war, and at my office goodbye party Nathaniel whispered to me, "I'm going to pray for your safety." I never forgot that. I always considered his prayers my good luck charm, and when I walked out of Beirut in one piece three years later, one of the first things I did was thank Nathaniel for keeping watch over me. He liked that a lot.

I only wish I could have returned the favor. You see, a few years later Nathaniel gave up editing and became a reporter himself, first in Argentina and then as the *Times*'s business reporter in Europe, based in Germany. Nathaniel was a wonderful reporter, and one of the most uncynical people I ever knew. Indeed, the book on Nathaniel as a reporter was that he was too nice. His colleagues always doubted that anyone that nice could succeed in journalism, but somehow he triumphed over this handicap and went from one successful assignment to another. This was because Nathaniel intuitively understood that there is a big difference between skepticism and cynicism. Skepticism is about asking questions, being dubious, being wary, not being gullible but always being open to being convinced of a new fact or angle. Cynicism is about already having the answers—or thinking you do—answers about a person or an event. The skeptic says, "I don't think that's true; I'm going to check it out." The cynic says, "I know that's not true. It couldn't be. I'm going to slam him." Nathaniel always honored that distinction.

Unfortunately, Nathaniel Nash, at age forty-four, was the sole American reporter traveling on Commerce Secretary Ron Brown's airplane when it crashed into a Croatian hillside in 1996. Always remember, real journalists are not those loudmouth talking heads you see on cable television. Real journalists are reporters, like Nathaniel Nash, who go off to uncomfortable and often dangerous places like Croatia and get on a military plane to chase after a visiting dignitary, without giving it a second thought—all to get a few fresh quotes, maybe a scoop, or even just a paragraph of color that no one else had. My prayers were too late for Nathaniel, but he was such a good soul, I feel certain that right now he's sitting at God's elbow taking notes—with skepticism, not cynicism. So be a skeptic, not a cynic. We have more than enough of those in our country already, and so much more creative juice comes from skepticism than from cynicism.

Whoopi Goldberg

Oscar, Grammy, Tony, and Emmy Award Winner

—————

Do Unto Others

My code—the one I try to live by but don't always succeed—is "Do unto others as you would have them do unto you." This applies anywhere. If you're walking down the street and hear someone's cellphone conversation and you're annoyed because she's talking way too loudly, or if you're in a restaurant and you hear someone speaking at the top of his lungs, chances are the next time you're on your cellphone, or at a diner, you might just drop your voice. Or when you're in an elevator and someone is a stink factory, and you're thinking, God, that woman is wearing way too much perfume, then perhaps the next time you put yours on you'll be more conscientious. If we carry this phrase, "Do unto others as you would have them do unto you," with us, we all might get through life a little bit easier.

PART 6

DON'T LET THE TURKEYS
GET YOU DOWN

On Rejection and Resilience

If I had listened to the critics I'd have died drunk in the gutter.

—ANTON CHEKHOV

If I thought I had experienced challenges early in my career, I hadn't seen anything yet. The time in my professional life that required every drop of resilience in my personal reservoir came during my first two years as the anchor of the *CBS Evening News*. There had been a great deal of hype over my hire. I was the first woman to solo-anchor an evening newscast on a major network, and the significance of that wasn't lost on me. In fact, when I was offered a job on the *Today* show fifteen years earlier I told Michael Gartner, then the president of NBC News, that I would accept the job only if Bryant Gumbel and I were going to be equal partners. I didn't want to be relegated to cooking and fashion segments, and I wanted assurances that that wouldn't happen. So in a moment of extreme moxiness I told him, "It's really important to me that there's a fifty-fifty division of labor." I had been covering the Pentagon and didn't want my news chops or credibility to be eroded. So he relented. Almost. "Fifty-two, forty-eight," he told me. "And that's my best offer." I agreed. I think I had the audacity to insist on an equal division of labor because I was well aware of how images from television can shape attitudes and values. God knows I was influenced by watching the adventures of a career woman named Mary Richards every Friday night on *The Mary Tyler Moore Show,* and by the show *Julia,* starring Diahann Carroll, about an African-American nurse and single mother.

When CBS came calling, I once again thought about the importance of seeing a woman in the role of solo anchor. I would be shepherding a broadcast that had been largely the domain of white males. That, coupled with the challenge of reinvigorating a genre that had a declining viewership, made the opportunity too exciting to pass up. But little did I know what lurked ahead.

As Linda Ellerbee once wrote, "Some days you're the pigeon, and some days you're the statue." Well, I was the statue for about two years, and let me tell you, it's not a lot of fun. From my very first day, I was pounded for everything from the color of my jacket (it was white, tropical-weight wool, and perfectly acceptable after Labor Day!) to my eye makeup and the way I held my hands. There had been a great deal of publicity before the first broadcast, and in the initial few weeks the ratings were high. But when they started to head south, it became open season for the critics. Despite fifteen years covering major news events and countless hard-hitting interviews, they claimed that I didn't have the "gravitas" (which I decided was the Latin word for *testicles*) required to be at the helm of such a prestigious enterprise. I often felt like the protagonist in T. S. Eliot's famous poem "The Love Song of J. Alfred Prufrock" when he spoke of "the eyes that fix you in a formulated phrase . . . pinned and wriggling on the wall." The very public vivisection was at times painful and hard to understand. During that dispiriting period, I often imagined one of the New York City buses with my face splashed across the side running me over on West Fifty-seventh Street. Somehow, it seemed a fitting O. Henry–esque ending to my current predicament. My sense of humor was getting pretty dark in those days.

My friends from NBC urged me to "come home." It was very tempting. Some days I just wanted to pull a Steven Slater, the fed-up JetBlue flight attendant who said, in so many words, "Take this job and shove it," before he slid down the escape chute. I found solace on, of all things, a coffee mug on a co-worker's desk that read, "Don't let the turkeys get you down." My friends were also great listeners and morale boosters. And I had many heart-to-heart conversations . . . with myself. "You've been successful before," I told myself. "You have something to offer. You haven't changed." I realized that whatever your path, whatever your calling, the most damaging thing you can do is let other voices define you and drown out your own. You've got to block them out and find that place deep inside you, shaken but still intact, and hold on to it. As many wise people have said, you can't always control the circumstances, but you can control how you repond to them. Even during those tough days, a voice inside me kept saying, "Keep going. You're in the big leagues. Put on your big-girl pants. You're not a quitter. There will be better days ahead." And there were. The broadcast got stronger, the team came together, and I got better. I fell back on my dad's advice: "Just do the best you can." And that's really the only thing we can all do, every day.

Kathryn Stockett
Bestselling Author of *The Help*

Don't Give Up, Just Lie

If you ask my husband what my best trait is, he'll smile and say, "She never gives up."

And if you ask him for my worst trait, he'll get a funny tic in his cheek and narrow his eyes and hiss, "She. Never. Gives. Up."

It took me a year and a half to write my earliest version of *The Help*. I'd told most of my friends and family what I was working on. Why not? We are compelled to talk about our passions. When I'd polished my story, I announced that it was done and mailed it to a literary agent.

Six weeks later I received a rejection letter from the agent, stating, "Story did not sustain my interest." I was thrilled! I called my friends and told them I'd gotten my first rejection! Right away, I went back to editing. I was sure that I could make the story tenser, more riveting, *better*.

Several months later, I sent it to a few more agents. And received a few more rejections. Well, more like fifteen. I was a little less giddy this time, but I kept my chin up. "Maybe the next book will be the one," a friend said. *Next* book? I wasn't about to move on to the next one just because of a few stupid letters. I wanted to write *this* book.

A year and a half later, I opened my fortieth rejection: "There is no market for this kind of tiring writing." That one finally made me cry. "You have so much resolve, Kathryn," a friend said to me. "How do you keep yourself from feeling like this has been just a huge waste of your time?"

That was a hard weekend. I spent it in pajamas, slothing around that racetrack of self-pity—you know the one, from sofa to chair to bed to re-frigerator, starting over again on the sofa. But I couldn't let go of *The Help*. Call it tenacity, call it resolve, or call it what my husband calls it: *stubbornness.*

After rejection number forty, I started lying to my friends about what I did on the weekends. They were amazed by how many times a person could repaint an apartment. The truth was, I was embarrassed for my friends and family to know that I was still working on the same story, the one nobody apparently wanted to read.

Sometimes I'd go to literary conferences, just to be around other writers who were trying to get published. I'd inevitably meet some suc-cessful writer who told me, "Just keep at it. I received fourteen rejections before I finally got an agent. *Fourteen!* How many have you gotten?"

By rejection number fifty-five, I was truly neurotic. It was all I could think about—revising the book, making it better, getting an agent, get-ting it published. I insisted on rewriting the last chapter an hour before I was due at the hospital to give birth to my daughter. I would not go to the hospital until I'd typed *The End*. I was still poring over my research when the nurse looked at me as if I weren't human and said in a New Jersey accent, "Put the book down, you nut job, you're *crowning*."

It got worse. I started lying to my husband. It was as if I were having an affair—with ten black maids and a skinny white girl. After my daughter was born, I began sneaking off to hotels on the weekends to get a few hours of writing in. "I'm off to the Poconos! Off on a girls' week-end!" I'd say. Meanwhile, I'd be at the Comfort Inn around the corner. It was an awful way to act, but—for God's sake—*I could not make myself give up.*

In the end, I received sixty rejections for *The Help*. Letter number sixty-one was the one that accepted me. After my five years of writing and three and a half years of rejection, an agent named Susan Ramer took pity on me. What if I had given up at fifteen? Or forty? Or even sixty? Three weeks later, Susan sold *The Help* to Amy Einhorn Books.

The point is, I can't tell you how to succeed. But I can tell you how not to: Give in to the shame of being rejected and put your manuscript—

or painting, song, voice, dance moves, [insert passion here]—in the coffin that is your bedside drawer and close it for good. I *guarantee* you that it won't take you anywhere. Or you can do what this writer did: Give in to your obsession instead.

And if your friends make fun of you for chasing your dream, remember—just *lie*.

Malcolm Gladwell

Bestselling Author and Writer for *The New Yorker*

—

Don't Turn on Your Greatest Asset

Most people, I realize, get advice from their parents. But my parents are of the type who let their actions, not their words, set the example. So I can't point to some pithy bit of wisdom passed down from my father or mother (except for my father's solemn warning to me, when I graduated from college, to steer clear of journalism).

But as a kid I was a great fan of the baseball writer Bill James, who once wrote something that has always stayed with me. It was about the hugely talented Montreal Expos teams of the late 1970s and early 1980s, which never quite fulfilled their potential. Finally, one of those teams confronted its failures and got rid of the player it felt was the culprit—the catcher Gary Carter. But, as James pointed out, Carter wasn't the reason for the team's failure at all. He was, in fact, the best player there. The Expos, in their moment of crisis and desperation, had—paradoxically—turned on their greatest asset. I was incredibly struck by that observation. And since then I've seen versions of this mistake played out again and again, both in my own life and in the lives of others—not to mention in the politics of countries. That which we do best is the most visible and the most scrutinized thing about us, so it is almost inevitable that when times get hard it's the aspect of our lives that we fixate on—for better (occasionally) but mostly for worse. I've seen relationships falter in bad times, not because they were weak but because they were strong. I saw this country, after 9/11, respond to a challenge to its values (freedom and tolerance) by attacking those very same values. And it's only by remembering that bit of advice from Bill James that I've prevented myself from making this same mistake again and again.

Carter is in baseball's Hall of Fame, by the way. Most of his teammates on the Expos have been long forgotten.

Davis Guggenheim

Academy Award–Winning Film Director and Producer

―――

Don't Listen to Can't

You've probably heard this one: "Don't let anyone tell you that you can't." It's a big theme in our household. Everything stops when we hear one of our kids say, "I can't." We all huddle together and have a big discussion about how anything is possible if you work hard and focus on your goal. But the problem with "Don't let anyone tell you that you can't" is that so many people in your life *do*. In my life, there were high-school guidance counselors, coaches, friends, and bosses, to name a few. I'm not suggesting that every naysayer is evil. I don't believe that. It's just that there are many good-natured types out there who are just doing their job, and in the process they might be saying, "You can't."

The truth is, on paper I was one of the most unimpressive kids around. I was a terrible student, listless and unfocused. When I told people that I wanted to become a director, it made sense that many thought, I'm doing this kid a favor if I "adjust" his expectations and point him toward a more "realistic" field. They wanted to let me down easy with well-intentioned advice, which basically amounted to "Don't reach so high." The great news is that I also had a few wonderful teachers and my parents, who saw past those low expectations and believed in me.

Here's my point: It's not about "not letting" people tell you that "you can't." My experience is that they will tell you that, anyway, and you can't stop them. So my advice is: Don't listen to them. If you have a strong desire and passion to do something, even when the smart advice is encouraging you to downgrade your expectations, I say don't listen. Believe in yourself, because with hard work, passion, and persistence you can do anything.

―――

Tyra Banks

Supermodel Turned Super Mogul, Chairwoman and CEO of Bankable

SMIZE . . . with Your Booty

On the first day of the ninth grade, a girl approached my awkward, skinny, weird-looking, big-foreheaded self and asked a question that would change my life forever:

"Are you a model?"

Modeling was the furthest thing from my mind at the time, but these four words piqued my interest and I went about getting signed. I studied my butt off to learn every element of the fashion industry. I researched, investigated, devoured books, magazines, and videos on designers, photographers, models—I took it all in!

After I graduated from high school, Paris was my destination. Terrified but filled with courage and ambition, I pushed through the fears and rejections, like "Sorry, Ms. Banks, we're not sure if you're photogenic." Or the one that I heard more than anything: "We already have a black girl."

But I kept going after each blow. Why? Because I was getting better and stronger, wiser and more passionate. And in the end my non-photogenic, already-have-a-black-girl, weird-looking-big-foreheaded self booked twenty-five fashion shows that season. My *first* season in Paris. I've been told that it was the first and last time a neophyte booked that many shows. And no, it wasn't because I had the right walk or the look of the moment. I believe I booked that record number of shows because of the studying I put in beforehand. I was prepared! I propelled and fueled my destiny with research, knowledge, and commitment.

Over the years, I became a full-fledged supermodel and accomplished everything that I dreamed of and more. But eventually I realized that I would need to make the ultimate tough decision to walk away from modeling before it "walked away from me." To retire on top. Then came the question:

"Now what?"

I had many conversations with myself in which I asked, "Tyra, what is your dream—the one thing over all others that you want to accomplish now?"

I answered that burning question with the ultimate, universal fantasy: to become a singing sensation. Oh, yes. I wanted to be a pop star! I recorded countless never-released songs and even self-produced a music video called "Shake Ya Body." Okay, truth be told I was less interested in actually recording music. All I really wanted to do was "shake my body" in music videos and onstage at Madison Square Garden. I wanted all the accolades, choreography, applause, and exclusive interviews. I even envisioned being interviewed by Katie Couric, who would ask, "Tyra, what was your *inspiration* for this album and the musical movement called SMIZE . . . with Your Booty?" And, with a hair flip and a twinkle of the eye, I'd reply, "Well, Katie, I've already conquered the *SMIZE*—smiling with the eyes, that is—in modeling, and now it's time for the entire world to experience this auditory masterpiece, and to embody the SMIZE of the cheeks—down there." Oh, I was *so ready.* Ready to *shine*! Thank God I spared Katie that horrible interview, because my nearly tone-deaf, pitchy, Auto-Tuned, have-access-to-the-best-producers-in-the-world-but-still-sucked-big-time SMIZING butt had to face the real music! I was not meant to be the next Lady Taylor Perry Gaga Swift.

Luckily for me, I faced the truth with honesty and let go of the fantasy of being a singing star. I realized that my joy and passion, combined with my all-consuming focus and work ethic, really was best suited for the world of business. The *business* side of Entertainment, the *business* side of Beauty, the *business* side of Fashion—meshed with all my right-brained strengths: creating, producing, writing! I am an entrepreneur. I am a businesswoman. That is in no way a fantasy; that is my destiny.

And so Bankable was born, and it has been my driving force. With the same commitment to hard work and study that led to my success in modeling, I attend Harvard Business School in order to make my company the best of the best, and to learn how to become a true leader in the world of beauty-meets-entertainment. Today, we're establishing an innovative and inspiring corporate culture that is vibrant, humorous, and highly creative. Our employees have fun and thrive, and our mantra is our mission: to truly expand the definition of beauty worldwide.

Now that's true destiny, no Auto-Tune required—just pure acoustic harmony.

Destiny is born out of our true gifts, which each of us must focus on, investigate, and invest in. It is not born out of foolish fantasy. As I've learned over the years, destiny can become reality only when we step back, examine ourselves and our motives, and think of what we are *truly* willing and capable of dedicating our soul, our spirit, our lives to.

So search for your own destiny—a destiny that's real—and make sure you master how to *SMIZE* with your booty while finding it.

Salman Rushdie

Bestselling, Award-Winning Author of Eleven Novels,
Including *Midnight's Children* and *Luka and the Fire of Life*

———

Angela's Asterisks

When I was a young, unpublished, struggling writer in London in the mid-1970s, I met the great British fantasist, feminist, eccentric, and all-around wonderful woman Angela Carter. She was the first writer who spoke to me as an equal, encouraged me to keep at my writing, and gave me a little much-needed self-belief. Her finest literary advice boiled down to five pithy words, one of them obscene:

"F*** the lot of them."

It is advice I have tried to follow ever since.

Colin Powell

Four-Star General and Sixty-fifth United States Secretary of State

_____

It Doesn't Matter Where You Start

I graduated from the City College of New York fifty-two years ago. They were glad to see me go, with my 2.0 average, hoping the Army could do something with me. I am now considered one of the greatest sons of City College and they name things after me. So it doesn't matter where you start in life but where you finish and, along the way, whether you do something that you love and enjoy doing. Never settle for anything less than what you love doing and do well.

Laura Linney
Award-Winning Film, Television, and Theater Actress

Never Read Your Own Reviews

In life, you will inevitably encounter criticism. Never, ever read your own reviews. Good ones or bad ones. It is not a critic's job to tell you how to feel about your own work. That is your responsibility alone. Never allow anyone to tell you how to feel about your work. Or limit your view of yourself or of who you are.

The most interesting artists are those who aren't too afraid to fail. As the late great Jack Lemmon once said, "Failure seldom stops you. What stops you is the fear of failure." You will never achieve a deeper understanding of your work, or learn the tough lessons, if you are liked or comfortable all of the time.

Martha Stewart

Lifestyle Expert, Bestselling Author, and Founder
of Martha Stewart Living Omnimedia

—

Gather the Good Things

So the pie isn't perfect? Cut it into wedges. When faced with a challenge, evaluate or assess the situation, gather the good things in sight, abandon the bad, clear your mind, and move on. Focus on the positive. Stay in control, and never panic.

M. Night Shyamalan
Filmmaker

Sadness

There is a book that has stayed with me, that has been able to express those feelings I am incapable of bringing forth into words.

The book is titled *Letters to a Young Poet,* and was written by Rainer Maria Rilke. Rilke wrote a series of letters to an aspiring young poet advising him on art and life. In reading it, as countless have, I felt that he was writing to me.

Of the nineteen quotes of his that I have written down in my notebooks, this one stirs me every time I read it:

> Perhaps we would bear our sadness with greater trust than we have in our joys. For they are the moments when something new has entered us, something unknown; our feelings grow mute in shy embarrassment, everything in us withdraws, a silence arises, and the new experience, which no one knows, stands in the midst of it all and says nothing.

When I am hurt—and that is often—I now try to see it as something other than pain.

When I am lost—and that is often—I remember to take a deep breath and look around to see the new place I am in.

I have always been okay with being vulnerable to the attacks of the world. However, as I grow older, I am getting weary. I have the urge to protect myself and not feel sadness with as much frequency as I have recklessly done in my youth.

This would be a mistake. Sadness has been misunderstood. Sadness is the soul recognizing change.

Soledad O'Brien

Award-Winning Journalist, Anchor, and Special Correspondent for CNN

Push Beyond Prejudice

One day, when I was in middle school, I was walking down the hall to my sixth-period science class when an older kid, an eighth grader, came up to me and said, "If you're a nigger, why don't you have big lips?" I remember trying to formulate an answer, as if the boy's question deserved a measured response. There was no hostility in his voice. It was just a question hurled at me in the rush to change class by a boy with long, sandy-brown bangs swinging in his eyes. I rushed past him. I just pursed my lips and kept moving.

I've always been proud of my heritage. I am the daughter of a black and Latina mother from Cuba and a white father from Australia. Both of my parents are immigrants. I was raised, with five brothers and sisters, to be proud of our cultural identity, but the issue of race never failed to stare me in the face. People did not see me in the way that I saw myself. I remember shopping at a store in our comfortable suburb of Smithtown, New York, and meeting a salesperson who explained that I "couldn't be black" because black people were thieves and killers. Um, gonna put this jacket down and leave now, I thought to myself. Then there was the clerk at a photo store where I went to get a picture taken with my sister. He asked if we were black and then apologized for asking, as if being African-American was an offense. My sister and I sped off. At school, being half black and half white meant that I was the brunt of too many bad jokes to count. I just turned and walked away. My young life seemed like a schoolyard game of dodgeball: If you stood still, you got hit. But if you moved you survived to play again.

I've been a journalist now for nearly twenty years. I often sprint from story to story, and my life moves fast. I am a big version of the little girl in Smithtown, except that now I'm walking toward something rather than away from it. Each day I force people to consider what they've said in interviews. I dig into the awkward questions. I revel in making people rethink their words. I've produced award-winning documentaries about challenging subjects like race, and have gone on to write books, give speeches, marry a great guy, have four healthy kids, and anchor a network TV show. That eighth grader in the hallway didn't hinder my forward motion. Whatever became of him, he was wrong about me. Whatever assumptions he made about me, I proved him wrong.

The important lesson, to me at least, is that I've succeeded in life despite the narrow-mindedness that I faced growing up. Dealing with prejudice actually changed me for the better, not for the worse. I learned that I didn't need to acknowledge—or give power to—every injustice thrown in my way. Instead, I could win just by being myself. Yes, I felt angry at the time, but I used the negativism as motivation and didn't let it fester. I realized that anger could teach me, and I've used those feelings in my work to identify with people—to say, "I've been there, too."

One thing that's certain in this country is that not far around the corner from every ugly experience is something really beautiful. And if you stop at every bitter comment you will never reach that beauty. My strategy has always been to push forward, to be proud, and to have faith in myself. In other words, never give intolerance the satisfaction of a backward glance.

PART 7

EVERYONE NEEDS A CHEERLEADER

On Mentors and Encouragement

No matter what accomplishments you make, somebody helps you.

—Wilma Rudolph

A husband and wife in their early sixties were celebrating their fortieth wedding anniversary in a romantic little restaurant. Suddenly, a tiny, beautiful fairy godmother appeared on their table. "For being such an exemplary and loving married couple all these years," she told them, "I will grant you one wish." The wife answered, "Oh, I want to travel around the world with my darling husband." The fairy waved her magic wand and—poof!—two tickets for the *Queen Mary 2* appeared in the wife's hand. The husband thought for a moment, then said, "Well, this is all very romantic, but an opportunity like this will never come again. I'm sorry, sweetheart, but my wish is to have a wife who's thirty years younger than me." The wife and the fairy were deeply disappointed, but a wish is a wish. So the fairy waved her magic wand and—poof!—the husband became ninety-two years old. The moral of this story: Men should remember that fairy godmothers are female.

I love telling this joke, because it never fails to make me appreciate the collective power of the many wonderful women in my life. As women, we are all each other's fairy godmother, watching over one another, suddenly appearing when we're in dire straits, coming up with something to wear to the ball or on a dreaded blind date, picking the best photo for—*horrors!*—Match.com. I know that without my girlfriends my life would not be as rich or as rewarding—or nearly as much fun.

But before all the men out there flip to the next chapter with a collective groan or head to a sports bar to drink a beer and watch a game, wait a second. While fairy godmothers may be female, sometimes the best cheerleaders are men. In my case, the most vocal supporter with the biggest megaphone was none other than Tim Russert, one of the finest people I have ever known. It was 1989, and I was still recovering from my disastrous on-air debut at WRC when Tim called upstairs to the local newsroom in Washington and said he'd like to see me in his office. Tim was, of course, the Washington bureau chief and beloved anchor of *Meet the Press.* It was a very exciting day. He told me that he admired my work, especially the way I'd hounded Marion Barry, the controversial mayor of Washington, D.C., at the time, "like a pit bull hot on the trail of an alley cat." He told me that I had spunk, and that, unlike Lou Grant, the gruff, cantankerous boss on *The Mary Tyler Moore Show,* Tim liked spunk. He offered me a job as a deputy Pentagon correspondent. Six months later, I was substitute-anchoring for the weekend edition of *NBC Nightly News.* Having Tim as my cheerleader was so meaningful— professionally and personally. Perhaps no one was more respected at NBC News than Tim—for his integrity, work ethic, and humility. His Buffalo roots were so integral to who he was, and he always thought about people like his dad, Big Russ, watching the show alongside inside-the-Beltway pundits and policy wonks. And his dogged preparation kept every politician on his or her toes, in a way that was appropriately challenging but never overly combative. He was the E. F. Hutton of NBC: When Tim talked . . . people listened. With him in my corner, opportunities started coming my way, and without those opportunities I would never be where I am today. When Tim died suddenly of a heart attack, it was the entire nation's loss.

The object lesson from this experience is this: It takes one person—

just one—to see something special in someone else, to lift her up and give her a chance. My mom used to say, "Everyone needs a cheerleader." In my career, that was Tim—he changed everything. So find yourself a cheerleader, and perhaps even more important, someone *you* can cheer for.

Christiane Amanpour

Award-Winning International-Affairs Journalist and Anchor

Thank You, Colonel Shaki

I first met Colonel Shaki when I was five years old, growing up in Tehran. A loud and colorful former cavalry officer in the Iranian Army, Colonel Shaki was my horseback-riding instructor and my earliest mentor. At my first lesson, the colonel did not start me off on a little pony, ambling around the ring on a long leash, as my parents and I had perhaps expected. Instead, he hoisted me onto a full-grown horse—gigantic to my five-year-old eyes—and expected me to stay in the saddle, or not! At first it was terrifying, trying to control a beast with a mind of its own. I hung on for dear life as the horse took off at a death-defying pace around the ring. All the while, Colonel Shaki shouted indecipherable instructions that I strained to hear, let alone understand.

I fell off, I cried, I looked to my mum for rescue. Colonel Shaki strode over. Phew, I thought, he'll give me a rest and a lollipop. No such luck. Suddenly he had me by the scruff of my neck and—plop!—I was back in the saddle. Over and over this happened. But I never gave up; I wasn't allowed to. My mother didn't step in to save me, and the colonel wasn't going to let me off the hook. Slowly but surely, I grew proficient, capable, in control. I got good at it. And, best of all, from fear and dread I grew to love it.

Riding taught me all that I needed to know about life, its good times and how to get through its hard times. It taught me about persistence, toughness, courage, and I learned never to see a setback as a failure. It taught me passion, it taught me to have the commitment to master a "trade," and, most of all, it taught me about compassion and shared endeavor. A rider does not ride alone; her horse is her teammate.

I learned these lessons from Colonel Shaki at his riding stables. You can learn them anywhere, and take them everywhere throughout your life.

Al Roker

Television Broadcaster and Weather Anchor

Willard's Way

My best advice came from my mentor and second dad, Willard Scott. In 1976, I was a rookie weatherman at WTTG-TV in Washington, D.C. At the time, nobody watched the station except for shut-ins, the demented, and folks who had passed on and left the TV on Channel 5.

One day, out of the blue, I got a call from the one person in D.C. who was bigger than the president: Willard Scott. This was before Willard joined the *Today* show. He was *the* local weatherman and personality in Washington. He was inviting me to dinner. Me? The weather guy at Channel 5? Willard was a legend, not only in Washington but in the TV weather community.

We went to Alfredo's La Trattoria on Wisconsin Avenue. People were coming up to him left and right and, God bless him, he would introduce me as if I was his professional equal. During that dinner I was given two pieces of advice by Willard that I live by to this day, more than thirty years later:

(1) Always be yourself. It may not be much, but it's all you've got. No one can take that away from you, if you don't let them. Trying to be someone you're not takes up too much energy and is no fun. Willard is a prime example of "what you see is what you get."

And (2) Never give up your day job. Willard was the king of multitasking. During his long career he was, simultaneously, the original Ronald McDonald and half of a great radio morning team, the Joy Boys. He was the local weatherman and owned a farm in Delaplane, Virginia, where he hosted birthday parties and sold eggs at a local department store, Woody's. But he always did the weather. Even when he got to the *Today* show, he never gave up his day job of doing the weather.

I try to emulate that advice. I try to be myself each day. For better or for worse, it's who I am. And no matter what else I do—executive-producing a TV series, hosting the Macy's Thanksgiving Day Parade, or anchoring *Wake Up with Al* on the Weather Channel, I will always do the weather on *Today*. It's the source from which all else springs.

For this advice, I will always be grateful to my Uncle Willard.

Wes Moore

Entrepreneur, Bestselling Author, and Youth Advocate

Have Faith, Not Fear

As I prepared to deploy to Afghanistan in 2005 with the 82nd Airborne Division, my grandparents handed me a Bible. The weathered leather Bible was used by my grandfather for more than fifty years during his ministerial career. It had guided him through some of the happiest and the most trying moments of his life. As I gratefully accepted this heirloom, they asked me to open the front cover.

On the first page, in my grandfather's eighty-six-year-old handwriting, now weakened by cancer, were four simple words: "Have faith, not fear." The strength of this advice, combined with the love behind the gesture, touched me deeply and would sustain me in the trying months ahead.

I spent the next year in the border region of Afghanistan and Pakistan, in a remote area called Khost, which months before I could never have identified on a map. This isolated outpost quickly became my home; the many Afghans whom I fought alongside, my friends; the soldiers I led and with whom I served, my brothers and sisters. All the while, the words of my grandparents came back to me: Have faith, not fear.

What my grandparents knew, and what I learned, is that we can be paralyzed by the unknown. We can languish and allow ourselves to be controlled by fear. I saw it often while deployed; my fellow servicemen and women would wear fatalistic expressions each time we left "the wire," hoping it wasn't their time to have their number called. However, for me faith was the antidote to that fear. Faith not just in myself but in something larger. It was this faith that allowed us to push through, without being stymied by potential consequences or paralyzed by what-ifs.

I carried that tiny, worn Bible in the left breast pocket of my battle dress uniform every time I prepared myself and my soldiers for a mission. And I have relied on those four words for strength and guidance every day, that same way, ever since. Have faith, not fear.

Alex Rodriguez
Professional Baseball Player

The Power of Words

Among the influential people in my life, the two who played pivotal roles in my success were my high school baseball coach and my mother.

The slightest words of encouragement can affect a child's self-confidence and motivation. By age nine, I was training rigorously for both baseball and basketball. Years later, at Miami's Christopher Columbus Catholic High School, I continued to pursue baseball, although I was rather discouraged about my future in the sport. The varsity baseball team was loaded with players, and I was advised to concentrate solely on basketball. As much as I enjoyed basketball, it was not my true passion. Thankfully, a number of people told me to follow my heart and not give up on baseball.

Coincidentally, I received an amazing opportunity during my sophomore year to attend Westminster Christian, a private high school in Florida that had one of the state's top baseball programs. Heading up the team was Coach Rich Hofman, who kindly assisted me in getting financial aid to attend the school.

I had just transferred and was still feeling a little insecure about my future. Coach Hofman said something to me that would change my life forever: "You need to have a really big summer and work especially hard, because in three years you will be the number-one pick in the major-league baseball draft . . . and soon after you'll be in the big leagues for a long time."

His words of encouragement had a profound effect on my future, and I vowed not to disappoint him. My determination soared, and at the end of my junior year I was encouraged to bypass senior year and go straight to the majors.

Off the field, there was no bigger coach in my life than my mother, who made tremendous sacrifices so that I could pursue my dreams. During the day she worked full-time as an immigration secretary, and in the evening as a waitress, where she would stand on her feet for hours each shift.

When she returned home, exhausted from a sixteen-hour workday, I would count her tips and massage her tired legs. To this day, I marvel at her ability to rise above her circumstances, and I remind myself of her sacrifices whenever I feel even slightly challenged. My mother taught me the importance of quiet sacrifice. In her case, words were few, but her love and dedication were infinite.

For me, these two figures embody the power of positive thinking and determination. My mother taught me about perseverance, while Coach Hofman's abounding encouragement gave me the ability to think without limitations. Perhaps even more critical, their two voices drowned out any discouraging influences around me and taught me to trust my inner voice.

Curtis Sittenfeld

Bestselling Author of *Prep*, *The Man of My Dreams*, and *American Wife*

―――

My Other (Less Neurotic) Half

Frank Conroy was the director of the Iowa Writers' Workshop when I was a graduate student there, and he was perfectly suited to the role: He was white-haired, unapologetically opinionated, a wonderful writer, and an often hilarious introducer of various visiting writers. He was also a talented jazz pianist, and among the legends that circulated about him—and this one was actually true—was that he'd once jammed with the Rolling Stones. In a graduate program populated mostly by over-educated and gossipy twentysomethings trying to become legitimate poets and novelists, Frank was funny, candid, and magnificently un-flappable.

Frank's sixty-fifth birthday occurred in January 2001, just before the start of my last semester in the workshop, and a few of us who had been his recent students decided to take a cake over to his office. As we ate slices, we prodded him—although I'm not sure all that much prodding was necessary—to share with us the wisdom of his years.

In class, Frank would dispense advice about writing that I still think of, but on this winter morning he spoke more generally: Time is like a wind tunnel, and the older you get the faster it seems to pass. Life really is about the simple pleasures, like a good nap or a hot bath. Then he said it, the thing I consider pretty much the best advice ever: Don't marry someone who's more neurotic than you.

At the time, I would have been delighted to marry someone more neurotic than I was, especially a fellow writer. I imagined intense con-versations about language, a shared skepticism toward the conventions of ordinary life, when in reality I now suspect that the greater likelihood would have been professional competition and frequent ego massaging. I'm quite sure that I could have been a wife who was willing to endlessly prop up my husband's sense of self, and it's hard to overstate how happy I am that I don't have to.

The only flaw with this piece of advice is that, in any couple, just one person can follow it. And a few years after leaving Iowa, when I found myself in a serious relationship with a smart and easygoing guy named Matt, I fretted about whether I should ever tell him what Frank had said. An additional problem was that I couldn't remember whether Frank meant that a writer should never marry someone more neurotic or that no one should—a crucial distinction. Sadly, Frank died in 2005, so I couldn't check. I stewed and wondered: Should I warn my boyfriend away from me, or did the fact that he was an academic and a reader but not a writer mean that we were in the clear? This was, of course, the version I chose to believe.

Nevertheless, around the time we got engaged I repeated Frank's words to Matt. My husband-to-be gave me a look of deep amusement. "Curtis," he said, "do you think I don't realize you're more neurotic than I am?" We were married in March 2008.

Jay Leno
Comedian and Host of *The Tonight Show*

In Defense of Class Clowns

I grew up in Andover, Massachusetts, and I was lucky enough to have really great teachers in high school. Mrs. Hawkes taught English and creative writing, and I had her for sophomore English class. One day, she stopped me in the hall and said, "Come here, Jay, I want to talk to you. I always see you fooling around in class and I hear you telling stories in the hallway, and people seem to be laughing. Why don't you write those stories down and I'll accept them for class credit?" I took her up on the offer, and for the first time in my life I actually enjoyed doing homework. Up to that point, I was the kind of kid who did only what I *had* to do. *Excuse me, is this going to be on the test?* That was my usual question. But for the first time in my life I cared about doing well at something for its own sake. I started writing funny stories. I wrote it all down, crossed it out, rewrote it, tried it again from another angle, and I'd find myself—rather than the usual forty-five minutes I spent on homework—actually spending three hours trying to get the story perfect. In class, Mrs. Hawkes asked me to read my story aloud, and I got a few laughs in the usual kid way. Afterward, she said, "Jay, have you ever thought about becoming a comedy writer?" Although I'd always been a show-off and a cutup, it had never occurred to me that you could make a living by writing comedy, and so Mrs. Hawkes's question really sort of changed my life. I thought, Here is something I'm learning in school that I can actually use for a practical purpose. I had no interest in algebra or trigonometry. I was dyslexic, so that stuff had no meaning for me. But here was something new that, wow, I actually enjoyed doing, and it didn't seem like homework at all, and I even got credit for it! It was a real turning point in my life.

Today, whenever I meet young people who are interested in something—anything—I try to encourage them. Because so many kids these days aren't interested in anything. They just sort of hop around from one thing to the next, or maybe they just zone out. So, whether it's photography or painting or whatever it is, I always try to encourage them in any way that I can, because that's what someone did for me.

Larry David

Writer, Actor, Comedian, and Producer

—

Curb Your Enthusiasm, Please

Throughout my life, I've learned a lot. Unfortunately, I've retained next to nothing. There is, however, one piece of advice, given to me by my uncle Julius when I was a mere tyke, that has resonated with me lo these many years. It is, of course, to always, no matter what the circumstances—I don't care if you've won the lottery—always be sure to curb your enthusiasm. Uncle Julius, who hated mankind more than I hate zucchini, said, "Nobody wants to see you jumping up and down and acting like an idiot. . . . Nobody! I'm not saying you can't be enthusiastic. Just do it in private." I couldn't agree more. Unabashed displays of enthusiasm are every bit as off-putting as watching a couple making out in public. Do you think Anne Frank appreciated it when Miep Gies, the woman who hid her, paid a visit, then couldn't stop yammering about how beautiful it was outside? "Oh my God, Anne, what a spectacular day! I took a hike, played with my dogs, and just got back from swimming." To which Anne replied, "With all due respect, Frau Gies, I'm glad you had fun. Now do me favor. Shut the hell up and get out of here."

Ellen Levine
Editorial Director of Hearst Magazines

―――

Get Over Yourself

Right out of college, I was lucky to get a job as a reporter at a big daily newspaper in New Jersey. My dream had always been to live the life of comic-book heroine Brenda Starr. And there I was, working nights on the police beat following mob murders in Fort Lee and working days interviewing celebrities or covering fashion shows.

One of my biggest thrills was spending a few hours alone with a young Dustin Hoffman chatting about his first hit, *The Graduate*. This was before publicists ruled Hollywood. Dustin was easy to find. Hours after his film opened in New York City, I just looked him up in the white pages. His New York number: 989-7261. Sitting with Dustin for three hours was a twenty-one-year-old's fantasy. After my story appeared, he sent a handwritten note detailing how much he liked the feature and inviting me to a cocktail party at his New York apartment.

Days later, a fashion designer sent a limo to chauffeur me to an interview with a young starlet. As a thank-you for that profile, I got a huge flower arrangement. Then the governor of New Jersey requested that I visit the official mansion to report on his family and their life at home.

All that flattery and partying with celebrities was inflating my ego. My boss decided that it was time to take me to the woodshed. In the kindest way, she lectured me on the facts of life. (No, not those facts!) Miriam Petrie, highest-ranking woman on the paper and divorced mother of two, laid it out. "Get over yourself," she said. "It's not about you.

"Don't ever sit down at the dinner table with the people you're assigned to report on," she continued. "Don't, even for an hour, forget who you are. You are not a guest. You are an observer. The celebs at the party don't think of you as a friend. The compliments they toss your way are investments they expect to be returned with positive publicity." Channeling the voice of the fabulous Dame Edna, Miriam reminded me that I was merely a tool, the gateway to burnishing their image.

Helen Gurley Brown, the remarkable editor who created the *Cosmopolitan* magazine empire, worried out loud that when she retired no one would ask her to lunch. With her "I'm just a little girl from Little Rock" intuition, she had figured out that the billion-dollar magazine she'd created was the power position. She knew that the next editor occupying that throne would get the bouquets. Of course, friends took her to lunch, but the magic wand she once held passed into the hands of her successor.

A media job puts you in a position of power. Most jobs do. But leave the seat of power and the praise and flattery stop. So Miriam's words— "Get over yourself"—set me straight at twenty-one. You are who you really are. You are not the title that is attached to your name.

Craig Ferguson
Comedian, Writer, Actor, and Host of *The Late Late Show*

———

Hurry Up and Take Your Time

Every year around Christmastime in the U.K., hundreds of shows play at theaters all over the country in a festival called Pantomime. This tradition is perhaps the most commercially successful form of theater in the world outside of Broadway and the West End.

In every town there is a production. In the larger cities, big theaters have TV stars and famous comedians and successful reality contestants appearing in the shows to cash in on their fleeting moments of fame. In the smaller towns, the shows are less elaborate but still as popular with local audiences. This is because they know what they're going to get. "Panto," as it is lovingly referred to by customers and players alike, is strongly traditional: usually an old fairy story like "Sleeping Beauty" or "Jack and the Beanstalk" with a couple of songs, a few dance numbers, a slapstick sketch, and some jokes as old as Britain itself. This mass pilgrimage to the theaters in December and January has the happy result of a breakout in employment among actors.

As a young comic, I showed a petulant disdain for this tradition, citing my groovy rebellion and self-proclaimed genius as reasons not to appear in a panto. However, even a young genius like I was then has to make a little money now and again, so it was with some shame that I accepted the part of the "comedy policeman" in the Stirling MacRobert Arts Centre production of *Aladdin* in 1987.

On the first day of rehearsal, I met the show's director, an elderly Cockney gent by the name of Dennis Critchley. Dennis had been a young comic during the heady days of Music Hall in Britain (much the same as vaudeville in the U.S.) and knew every hackneyed old panto routine in the book. He assigned me a tried-and-true slapstick sketch called "Widow Twankee's Take Away." The sketch contained all the moments I had seen a thousand times myself as a child when I attended these shows on school trips or with my parents. I would get a custard pie in the face; I'd have seltzer squirted down my pants; I'd be outwitted by a piece of fur on a wire that was meant to be a rogue ferret; and I'd have to shoot a sausage that was trying to escape my custody. If you ever watch my TV show, you'll see that much of this material is still gleefully incorporated into my life. (The dancing horse Secretariat is a direct lift from panto.)

My comedy career up to this point had been all stand-up, cracking wise in nightclubs to other angry young drunks like myself. I had never been faced with physical comedy, and as rehearsals progressed it became evident that I was floundering. I could never get the seltzer/custard-pie/sausage flow that the routine required to be funny. I was infuriated and humiliated and embarrassed, and when geniuses are embarrassed they start looking for excuses and a way out.

Lucky for me, Dennis—the grand old master, the Yoda of the soda syphon, the Mr. Miyagi of the comedy sausage—had dealt with insecure young comics before. He took me through the routine inch by inch, step by step, and slowly we built speed and flow into what I now realize was more like a dance routine than anything else.

Over and over, he stressed the importance of pacing.

"Hurry up and take your time," he would say whenever I botched a maneuver or tripped over myself.

"What the hell does that even mean, Dennis?" I growled at him after a few days.

"Exactly as it says," he reiterated in his cartoon Cockney accent. "Take the time that you need, don't rush, but don't dawdle. It's your time; don't let your nerves f*** it up for you."

"You a philosopher, too?" I snarked.

"Exactly. Everything in life, young un. Hurry up and take your time. Now come on, you shot the sausage too early and your trousers are dry. Let's try again."

Every time I'm a little nervous about performing—most recently, just before going onstage for the second of two sold-out shows at Carnegie Hall in New York City—I remember the advice I got from the old English vaudevillian, who, of course, I grew to adore.

"Hurry up and take your time."

Not a bad philosophy for life, I've found.

Take that, Descartes.

Maria Elena Salinas

Emmy Award–Winning Univision News Anchor and Syndicated Columnist

----

You Never Stop Learning

My mother's wisdom is the compass that has guided my life. A Mexican immigrant, she taught me to embrace family values long before they became a political issue. She taught me to embrace two cultures, two languages, and two sets of traditions, and that you can be a working mother without sacrificing family life.

Tony DeMarco, a family friend who was better known as baseball player Fernando Valenzuela's manager, was the first person to put a microphone in my hand. "Don't sound like an announcer," he'd say. "Just be you." Years later, Paco Calderon, my old editor from Ecuador, echoed that lesson. Paco would tell me that the most important thing on television was to be natural, but this was also the most difficult thing to accomplish.

My first news director, Pete Moraga, loved to say that he could teach people how to read and write the news, but he couldn't teach them how to read and write. I remember a local election that I covered as a young reporter in Los Angeles. It was the first time a Latino was running for the City Council in decades. Latinos at that time made up twenty-five percent of the population yet had no political representation. I went out to interview people on the street about the election, and out of sixteen Hispanics with whom I spoke fifteen were not voting because they could not, didn't know there was an election going on, or simply weren't interested. When I returned to my newsroom and told Pete Moraga that I couldn't do the story with those results, he said, "Can't you see it? Your story is right there in front of you. This is the first time Latinos have an opportunity to elect one of their own, yet they're losing it because they feel disenfranchised from the political system." This piece of advice helped shape what would become a mission in my career: to work toward the political empowerment of the Latino community.

This leads me to possibly the best and most important piece of advice I ever got. My father, a simple man who was an intellectual, spoke six languages and had a doctorate degree in philosophy. He would walk around with a book in hand at all times. As a little girl, I asked him one day what he was doing, and he replied, "Studying." "Studying at your age?" I asked. He said, "Of course. You never stop learning."

Mo'Nique
Oscar-Winning Actress and Comedian

Not Going Through It . . . Growing Through It

One of the most profound lessons I've learned is that in life we don't go through things; we grow through them.

The decision to lose weight has been the most difficult yet rewarding challenge of my life. At my heaviest, 262 pounds, I was comfortable and content. Until then, I'd made a great living extolling the virtues of being Big and Beautiful. Having those extra pounds never prevented me from doing anything. In fact, it propelled me. And enabled me to connect with women who, like me, were told that they didn't matter. If I could be their champion, the one they could look to and say, "She's sexy, she's successful, and she's happy," then that's who I wanted to be. And I was great at it.

Then one day my husband, Sidney, sat me down in the quiet of our home and said, very frankly, "Mama, that's too much weight—I want you for a lifetime." Suddenly, fear set in. How on earth could I lose weight and still be true to the person I'd become? I fought. I cursed. I didn't want to do it. But I knew I had to. That's when I took a trip into my closet, the place I often visit to talk to the Universe. We had some serious discussions that usually started with me explaining why I couldn't do it and the Universe admonishing me for surrendering.

See, I've always been great at dispensing advice but not so good at accepting it. It was never my goal to become skinny, just healthy. The challenge to lose sixty-two pounds was more than a notion because I'm a chewer. Always have been, and I still love good food. But I had to change, even when the Nacho Cheese Doritos seemed to constantly call my name.

I started out walking, worked my way up to a personal trainer, then took dance and boxing classes, and gradually changed my diet. Someday, I'll run a marathon, I swear. But for now I'm happy with the results.

As the weight began to come off, a funny thing happened. The fear shifted. Anxiety turned into excitement, then enthusiasm, and finally courage as I shared my struggle publicly. The very people I was nervous about disappointing began to encourage me, and their lives improved, too. The beautiful thing was we were doing it together. Shedding the weight was the beginning of conquering other struggles, and it's led me to finally live up to my true purpose.

"Not Going Through It . . . Growing Through It" is now a life principle, a mantra happily shared. It's a lesson from a husband who cared enough to tell the truth, and a Universe that loves enough to demonstrate just how rich life can be when we obediently grow through it.

Melinda Gates

Founder and Co-Chair of the Bill & Melinda Gates Foundation

———

The Sky's the Limit

Growing up, I attended an all-girls high school in Dallas, Texas. My favorite teacher was named Mrs. Bauer, and one day she made a decision that changed my life.

In the fall of 1980, at the Texas State Mathematics Conference, Mrs. Bauer tried out a new gadget called a personal computer. Her first thought was "These are going to be big. We have to get them for the girls." My school's administrators agreed, but they asked, "How are we going to teach the girls to use computers?" Mrs. Bauer answered, "I will learn, so that I can teach them."

She promptly enrolled in a master's-degree program in computer science. She paid the tuition out of her own pocket, and drove herself more than a half hour to class every night after a full day of teaching math. All the while, she was raising three sons. It was a sacrifice, but it helped my classmates and me immeasurably.

Because of what Mrs. Bauer taught us about computers, my classmates and I were able to overcome the stereotype that girls can't excel at science and math. When I got to college, I had the confidence to enroll as the only girl in most of my computer-science classes. Later, I brought that self-assurance with me when I started work at Microsoft, even though I was the only woman among my peers.

The truth is that women can't prove they have equal ability until they have equal opportunity. That's what Mrs. Bauer gave all of us: the opportunity to show what we were capable of doing. When you have a mentor who puts no limits on your potential, the future starts to look a lot bigger and more exciting.

But Mrs. Bauer did more than just stoke a young woman's passion for computer science. She showed me what it means to make sacrifices to help others. She was always looking for another opportunity to serve, not because it was convenient for her but because she could see that the people around her needed help. As Mrs. Bauer showed me, if you give all your energy to everything you do, you will have a huge impact on the lives you touch.

That lesson has been precious to me. I remember it when I'm doing work on behalf of the Bill & Melinda Gates Foundation, and I try to pass Mrs. Bauer's example and wisdom on to my own children.

PART 8

LOOK OUTSIDE YOURSELF

On Commitment and Contribution

The key to a happier world is the growth of compassion. We do not need to become religious, nor do we need to believe in an ideology. All that is necessary is for each of us to develop our good human qualities.

— THE DALAI LAMA

Giving back has become part of my DNA, but it's a trait that's the result of nurture, not nature. My mom insisted that we volunteer at the Columbia Lighthouse for the Blind Summer Day Camp in Washington, D.C., throughout our high school years. It was one of the most formative and character-building experiences I've ever had. There were kids all over the Washington area at the camp, from very different socioeconomic backgrounds. I was first exposed to the group when my sister Kiki directed a camp production of *Peter Pan.* I was ten years old at the time, and watching an all-blind cast (Stuart Abramowitz as Peter, Tori Grenier as Wendy) accompanied by a totally blind piano player (Linda Kipps) was one of the most moving and inspiring things I had ever witnessed. I was so proud of the actors, and even prouder of my sister, and I couldn't wait to be a counselor myself.

During the course of three years, we went to the Smithsonian Folk-life Festival, took the campers swimming and bowling, and got relief from the muggy Washington summers with a giant parachute. My group of nine-year-olds started a band. I played the piano—mostly Scott Joplin—while they played the maracas, the bongos, or strummed a guitar. I'll never forget John Lee saying to me as he sat on top of the piano, "Miss Katie, play 'The Entertainer'! Play 'The Entertainer'!" I also remember having to put ointment in the eyes of a little French boy who had glaucoma—a task that required a strong stomach and maturity that I didn't think I had. Being with these kids and taking them on all kinds of adventures really opened my eyes, pun intended. It started me on the path of understanding a bigger world beyond Fortieth Street and York-town High School in Arlington, Virginia.

Today, my true calling is something that touched me so personally, as is often the case for people who champion a cause. After my husband, Jay, died of colon cancer, I felt a moral obligation to inform people about this second leading cancer killer of men and women. I asked my executive producer at the time, Jeff Zucker (a colon-cancer survivor himself), if I could do an on-air colonoscopy on the *Today* show. He said yes without skipping a beat. Since colon cancer has a better than ninety percent cure rate if detected early, and so many people do not get screened, I wanted to demystify and de-stigmatize the procedure. So I invited an NBC crew to watch me drink a gallon of that inappropriately named prep Go Lightly, and the next day to accompany me to Columbia Presbyterian Hospital, where a wonderful doctor, Kenneth Forde, got up close and personal and did the procedure. At one point, loopy on anesthesia, I believe I announced that I had a "pretty little colon." We reached a large audience, and colonoscopy screenings increased by twenty percent. Researchers at the University of Michigan call it the Couric effect. I prefer to think of it as the Jay Monahan effect.

I've had quite a career in television but, of all my professional accomplishments, my continued advocacy for cancer research and awareness has been by far the most meaningful. If that is my legacy and, in absentia, Jay's, then we've left a small imprint on the world by helping some people I'll never meet live longer, healthier lives.

One of the best endorsements of my work came out of nowhere ten years ago. My daughter Ellie, who was then nine, looked at me in the kitchen and said, "Mom, I'm really proud of the work you're doing with colon cancer." It almost took my breath away.

Stand Up to Cancer is another proud accomplishment. Eight women, many of them Hollywood powerhouses, and I started a grass-roots movement that has so far raised $180 million to support dream teams of cancer researchers from different institutions. Hell hath no fury like some pissed-off women who want to see more progress made against this insidious disease.

My daughters have learned the value of giving back as well. Lemonade stands for cancer research from the time they were in preschool, tutoring children who need some extra help, serving the homeless at the Bowery Mission—giving back has become a part of their DNA as well. But they get as much as they give. Carrie and I both tutor sixth graders at the Harlem Village Academy; it's something the two of us do together on Saturday mornings. One Friday night, I was ambivalent about keeping our weekend tutoring date. "Mom," Carrie admonished me, "you can't do that. We've made a commitment, and we have to follow through!" I'm amazed at how much they teach me every day.

Ken Burns

Emmy Award–Winning Director and Producer

Do Something Lasting

Many, many years ago, not long after I graduated from college, while working on my first film on the history of the Brooklyn Bridge and its great designer John A. Roebling, I decided—rather rashly—that I had to interview the now late playwright Arthur Miller, and he had, after several pleading phone calls from me, rather reluctantly agreed. Miller had, of course, written a play called *A View from the Bridge,* and I was sure that he would be able to shed some light on what I had come to believe was the greatest suspension bridge in the world—that remarkable amalgam of stone and steel, which after its improbable and dramatic construction became a source of sublime inspiration to artists and poets, photographers and filmmakers for more than a century.

But on the way to Miller's Connecticut farm I had picked up a copy of the play and discovered to my horror that there was not a single mention of the bridge—it was merely the background for a drama completely unrelated to the themes of my film. I was mortified, and it seemed only a few panic-stricken minutes later that we pulled into his drive and I nervously rang the great man's door.

The first thing a very tall and very imposing and very gruff Arthur Miller said to me when he opened the door was "You know, I don't know a damn thing about the Brooklyn Bridge. I can't help you."

I had been standing there for several moments in abject shame and utter humiliation when he finally relented and said, "Okay. Perhaps I can give you something. Come with me." Now, I had been planning to set up an elaborate interview around a favorite chair in his house, to take several hours to adjust the lighting, and to film several rolls, but Miller directed me to his backyard, where the late-afternoon shadows of a perfect fall day were lengthening. "Let's go—now," he said, and we all knew that he meant it. Clearly, in his mind this was not going to waste any more of his time than need be—and we weren't going to be staying long, either.

We scrambled to take a quick light reading, and put the 16-mm camera up on the tripod. There were only a few minutes left on the roll of film that was still in the magazine from the morning's shoot. The sound man fumbled with his reel-to-reel tape recorder, checking the levels. But now Miller refused even to sit down. He would do the interview standing up or not at all, and we scrambled to find an apple crate that I could stand on to approximate his height—but, of course, never his stature. "Let's go—now," he said again, clearly impatient with our, in retrospect, utter ineptitude. And we were completely flabbergasted; we had never done an interview where the subject wasn't quietly posed in some study or living room. My heart was pounding out of my chest; I can still remember the nausea I felt.

To this day, I do not remember what feeble question I asked him to get him to speak. It doesn't really matter now, I suppose, but Miller's few-sentence answer constituted the sum total of the interview, and it has stayed with me, like the panic, the rest of my life. I know it by heart. He said, "You see, the city is fundamentally a practical, utilitarian invention—and it always was. And then suddenly you see this steel poetry sticking there and it's a shock. It puts everything to shame and makes you wonder what else we could have done that was so marvelous and so unpresumptuous. It carries its weights, it does what it's supposed to do and yet . . . I mean they could have built another Manhattan Bridge and [Roebling] didn't. He really aspired to do something gorgeous. So it makes you feel that maybe you, too, could add something that would last and be beautiful."

That was the whole interview. "Maybe you, too, could add something that would last and be beautiful." Those words became the final words of my very first film and, in a way, they became—like the declaration of principles the young and still idealistic Charles Foster Kane tacks to the wall in Orson Welles's great masterpiece *Citizen Kane*—my guiding principle as well.

I'm not sure how well I've lived up to the creed Arthur Miller so generously gave me that afternoon, but his words still resonate for me every day: Do something that will last and be beautiful. It doesn't have to be a bridge—or a symphony or book or a business. It could be the look in the eye of a child you raise or a simple garden you tend. Do something that will last and be beautiful.

Jacqueline Novogratz
Founder of Acumen Fund and Bestselling Author of *The Blue Sweater*

____

Commit to Something Bigger Than Yourself

When I was attending Stanford's Graduate School of Business, I had the great fortune to meet John Gardner, a man of tremendous accomplishment, integrity, and humility. He had served with President Johnson as Secretary of Health, Education, and Welfare, founded the grassroots organization Common Cause, been president of the Carnegie Foundation, and established other important institutions, like the White House Fellows and the Independent Sector. Throughout his life, John focused not on his career but on how he could position himself to serve others in the world. I adored John, wanted to be like him, and believe it is one of my life's greatest blessings to have been mentored by him.

Years later I was offered a "once-in-a-lifetime career opportunity," complete with an exalted title, salary, and access to powerful people in the political realm. When I asked John for his advice, he listened carefully and then looked me straight in the eye. "I can see why you're tempted," he said, "and this job will certainly make you more interesting to others. But that's the wrong reason to accept a position. Instead, you should focus on being interested rather than interesting. Now, tell me how this job will truly give you a chance to serve others rather than a chance to serve your own career."

I didn't take the job. And I've never forgotten John's sage advice to focus on being interested rather than interesting. Fifteen years later, I understand his wisdom: a focus on being interested in others is the very foundation for a life of meaning and purpose.

John frequently reminded me to commit to something bigger than myself. "Commitment will set you free," he would say with a knowing look. As a young person, I didn't fully comprehend this, for I liked keeping my options open. I soon realized, though, that if you always keep your options open you end up living life with a lot of options but without anything of real value, whether in your profession, your family, or your community work.

Through founding Acumen Fund, a nonprofit organization that invests in entrepreneurs in order to bring affordable services like water, health care, clean energy, and housing to the poor, I've come to understand the power of commitment in the deepest sense. By committing to something bigger than myself—the goal of ending poverty—I've discovered a profound sense of meaning as well as a path to becoming my truest self. Indeed, the more rooted I feel by focusing on one big idea and one organization, the freer I am to explore many parts of that idea. This sense of freedom has enabled me to experience the human journey in ways that I otherwise could not have imagined.

John died a number of years ago, and through his death I've learned that the best legacy we can build is to give to others. Through me, and literally thousands like me, John is alive in the world. And as his mentees impart his wisdom to the next generation, so will his spirit thrive and continue to enrich and inspire. His life was a model not only because of what he did but because he made the world a better place just by being in it.

Meryl Streep

Academy Award–Winning Actress

Empathy Opens Doors

I remember very clearly my first conscious attempt at acting. I was six years old, placing my mother's half slip over my head in preparation to play the Virgin Mary in our living room. As I swaddled my Betsy Wetsy doll, I felt quieted, holy. My transfigured face and demeanor—captured on Super 8 by my dad—pulled my little brothers Harry (playing Joseph) and Dana (a barnyard animal) into the trance. They were drawn into the Nativity scene by the intensity of my focus, in a way that my usual technique for getting them to do what I wanted (yelling at them) never would have achieved.

Later, when I was nine, I took my mother's eyebrow pencil and carefully drew lines all over my face, replicating the wrinkles that I had memorized on the face of my grandmother, whom I adored. I made my mother take my picture, and when I look at it all these years later I see myself now and my grandmother then. I remember in my bones how it was possible on that day to feel her age. I stooped, I felt weighted down but cheerful; I felt like her. Empathy is the heart of the actor's art.

In high school, another form of acting took hold of me. I wanted to learn how to be appealing. I studied the character I imagined I wanted to be: that of the generically pretty high school girl. I researched her deeply—that is to say, shallowly—in *Vogue, Seventeen,* and *Mademoiselle.* I tried to imitate her hair, lipstick, lashes, the clothes of the lissome, beautiful, superficially appealing high school girls I saw in those pages. I ate an apple a day. Period. I peroxided my hair, ironed it straight. I demanded brand-name clothes (my mother shut me down on that end). I worked harder on this characterization than on any one I've done since.

I worked on my giggle. I lightened it, and liked it more when it kind of went up? At the end? Because I thought it sounded childlike and cute. This was all about appealing to boys and, at the same time, being accepted by the girls. (A tricky negotiation—often, success in one area precludes succeeding in the other.) Along with the exterior choices, I worked on my—what actors call—interior adjustment. I adjusted my natural temperament, which tended—tends—to be slightly bossy, opinionated, a little loud, full of pronouncements and high spirits; and I *willfully* cultivated softness, agreeableness, a natural breezy sort of sweetness, even a shyness, if you will, which was very, very, very effective. On the boys. The girls didn't buy it. They didn't like me. They sniffed it out, the acting. (They were probably right.) But I was committed. This was absolutely not a cynical exercise. It was a vestigial survival courtship skill I was developing. I reached a point, senior year, where my adjustment felt like me. I had convinced myself that I was this person, and she me. Pretty, talented, but not stuck-up, a girl who laughed— a lot, at every stupid thing every boy said—and lowered her eyes, at the right moment, and deferred; who learned to defer when the boys took over the conversation. I remember doing this. I could tell that I was much less annoying to the guys than I had been; they liked me better, and I liked that. This was conscious but at the same time motivated and fully, fully felt. This was real acting.

I got to Vassar, which forty-three years ago was a single-sex institution like all the colleges in what were called the Seven Sisters, the female Ivy League. I made some quick but lifelong, challenging friends. With their help, and outside any competition for boys, my brain woke up. I got up and outside myself, and found myself again. I didn't have to pretend. I could be goofy, and vehement, and aggressive, and slovenly, and open and funny and tough, and my friends let me. I didn't wash my hair for three weeks once. They accepted me. Like the Velveteen Rabbit, I became real, instead of an imaginary stuffed bunny.

I stockpiled that character from high school and breathed life into her years later as Linda in *The Deer Hunter,* a film co-starring Robert De Niro and Chris Walken that won Best Picture in 1978. I played Linda, a small-town girl from a working-class background. A lovely, quiet, hapless girl who waited for the boys she loved to come home from the war in Vietnam. Often, men my age mention that character as their favorite of all the women I've played. I have my own secret understanding of why that is, and it confirms all my high school decisions. This is not to denigrate that girl, or the men who were drawn to her, in any way. She is still a part of me. She was not acting, but she was behaving in the way that cowed girls, submissive girls, beaten-up girls with few ways out have behaved since forever—and still do, in many worlds.

Now, as a measure of how much the world has changed, the character most men mention as their favorite is Miranda Priestly, the beleaguered totalitarian at the head of *Runway* magazine in *The Devil Wears Prada.* To my mind, this represents a huge change. They relate to Miranda. They wanted to date Linda. They felt sorry for Linda, but they *like* Miranda. They can relate to her issues: the high standards she set for herself and others, the thanklessness of the leadership position. The "nobody understands me" thing—the loneliness. They stand outside one character and pity her (and fall in love with her); they look through the eyes of the other. This is such a big deal because, as people in the movie business know, the most difficult thing in the world is to persuade a straight male audience to identify with a woman protagonist, to feel themselves embodied by her. This, more than any other factor, explains why we get the movies we get, and the paucity of roles in which women drive the film.

It's easier for the female audience. We've grown up identifying with male characters from Shakespeare to Salinger. We have less trouble following Hamlet's travails viscerally, or Romeo's or Tybalt's, or those of Huck Finn or Peter Pan or the Lion King or the boys in *Toy Story.* But it's much, much harder for heterosexual boys to be willing to identify with Juliet or Desdemona or Ophelia or Wendy in *Peter Pan* or Jo in *Little Women,* the Little Mermaid or Pocahontas. Why? I don't know. It just is. There has been a resistance to imaginatively assuming another persona if it is a "she."

But things are changing. Men are adapting, consciously and also without realizing it, for the better of the whole group. They are changing their deepest prejudices to accept and regard as normal things their fathers would have found very, very difficult, and their grandfathers would have abhorred. And the door to this emotional shift is empathy. As Jung said, "Emotion is the chief source of all becoming-conscious. There can be no transforming of darkness into light and of apathy into movement without emotion."

What I do know about "success," fame, and celebrity would fill volumes. How it separates you from your friends, reality, proportion, your own sweet anonymity (a treasure that you don't even know you have until it's gone). How it makes things tough for the family. Whether being famous matters one bit, really, in the end, in the ongoing flux of time. I have won a long list of awards, and while I'm very proud of the work, I can assure you that awards have very little bearing on my personal happiness and sense of purpose and well-being. That comes from studying the world feelingly, with empathy in the work. It comes from staying alert and involved in the lives of those I love and of those in the wider world who need my help. No matter what you hear me say when I'm holding a statuette on TV, and crying and spewing, *that* is acting. Being a celebrity has taught me to hide. But being an actor has opened my soul.

John Wood

Founder and Board Chairman of Room to Read,
Author of *Leaving Microsoft to Change the World*

———

Not Every Path Should Be Linear

We live in a world that has a lot of predefined notions of success. We are supposed to study hard, get good grades, go to the best university, work for a prestigious firm—the list goes on. Societal expectations can be good for us by pointing the way forward. But they also risk becoming a straitjacket that stifles creativity.

I was on such a path throughout the first fifteen years of my life after high school. Intent on "proving myself" at a young age, I was lucky enough to join Microsoft back in 1991, when it was still a small and young company. I rose through the ranks over the course of a fast-moving decade. Living overseas, I had it all: first-class round-the-world airline tickets, a fully subsidized house in Beijing, two housekeepers, and a car with a full-time driver. What I was beginning to lack, however, was passion. I felt that my life was devoted to making rich people richer. At age thirty-four, I asked myself, Is this all there is?

I had the good fortune one day to discover a potential nonlinear path. As an escape from my job, I decided to make a solo trek through the Himalayas—an eighteen-day, two-hundred-mile journey along Nepal's famous Annapurna Circuit. For months leading up to the trip, I fantasized about being out in the crisp, clean mountain air, trekking as high as eighteen thousand feet among glaciers and yaks. But on day two of my trek life threw something in my path that would change my course forever.

Along the trail, I met the headmaster of a local school. He invited me to visit the school to meet some of his 450 students. I felt excited, thinking this was a chance to see the real Nepal, not the tourist's version. The school itself wasn't much to speak of—mud walls, a leaky sheet-metal roof, and dirt floors. The students didn't have desks, and the chalkboard was the size of a postage stamp. But what really struck me was the school's "library." A library in name only, it was an empty room utterly devoid of books.

"Why?" I asked the headmaster. "How can you have four hundred and fifty students and yet not have something as fundamental as books?"

His answer hit me hard. "We are too poor to afford education in Nepal," he said sadly. His face dropped and his eyes dulled as he finished the thought: "But until we have education we will always be poor."

It struck me that the headmaster's lament said more about global poverty than any fancy academic report ever could. I had traveled enough to know that the billion people in this world living on less than a dollar a day aren't dumb, nor are they lazy. They are simply caught in this trap of being too poor to afford education, but without it . . .

It was on that day that the idea for Room to Read was born. Within two months, I had started a book drive, and soon thereafter I quit my executive position at Microsoft to create an organization that would bring thousands, and ultimately millions, of books to eager young students like those in Bahundanda, Nepal. A lot of people told me that I was crazy to give up millions of dollars in stock options to devote my life to this cause, but I reminded myself that "nobody ever erected a statue in honor of a critic." It's so easy to criticize. It's much harder to build. But, ultimately, it's only the builders who matter.

Had I chosen to stay on my comfortable linear path in life, Room to Read would never have been established. Instead, because I chose to go nonlinear, more than five million children today have access to the ten thousand libraries we've opened during our first decade in operation.

I don't believe that people should *always* follow nonlinear paths. If you constantly go nonlinear, you might end up running around in a random pattern and failing to accomplish anything of significance. But if you go only linear in life, you might suffer that worst of all fates: being boring, and never knowing what might have been possible if you'd taken a risk. And, believe me, the world has enough boring adults.

So that is the challenge. It's knowing when to go linear. And when to go nonlinear. There is a time for each in life.

Lisa Ling

Oprah Winfrey Show Correspondent and Executive Producer
and Host of *Our America with Lisa Ling*

Give of Yourself

As a journalist, I have seen things that have scarred me. I have interacted with people who have haunted me. I have heard things that have pained me. As a result, I have long struggled with the notion of faith. I have said more times than I can count, "If there is a God, how can he allow this to happen? How can he let so many people suffer?"

Several years ago, I married a man of strong faith. One day he sent an email to me that said this: "On a street corner I saw a cold, shivering girl in a thin dress, with no hope of a decent meal. I got angry and said to God, 'Why did you permit this? Why don't you do something about it?' God replied, 'I certainly did something about it. I made you.'"

Whenever I start to blame God for what I encounter in the world, I stop and remind myself that maybe it is I who should be doing more. We get so hung up on the notion of success that we can easily forget about being of service to others. I have actually found that giving of oneself is far more fulfilling than gifting oneself.

Maggie Doyne

Founder of Kopila Valley Children's Home and blinknow.org

Everything You Need Is Everything You Have

After my senior year of high school, as my friends were heading off to college, my parents dropped me off at Newark Airport, where I boarded a plane and set off to travel the world. It was just me and my backpack on my first solo trip away from home. Four countries and twenty thousand miles later, I was trekking through the Himalayas in war-torn Nepal, where I began to meet hundreds of orphaned children. I fell in love with their bright eyes and beautiful smiles but was shocked to see them barely surviving without the most basic things that I had grown up with: a safe home, food, clothing, and the chance to go to school. The violent ten-year civil war, widespread disease, and extreme poverty have left an estimated forty-five thousand orphan children in Nepal to fend for themselves.

I distinctly remember the moment I decided to stop feeling guilty and helpless and do something. On a ramshackle bus ride through the most poverty-stricken villages in the region, I thought of the children who I knew would be trafficked, exploited, and sold as slaves. From a tiny roadside phone booth, I called my parents and asked them to wire over my life savings—five thousand dollars in babysitting money. After months of research and negotiations and a lot of hard work, I bought my first piece of land on the outskirts of a beautiful village in the midwestern border region of Nepal.

One year later, I officially opened the front door of Kopila Valley Children's Home, which was built brick by brick, by me and the local community in Nepal. There are now thirty-five children living in our cozy, cheerful home. In the spring of 2010, another of my dreams came true: Kopila Valley Primary School. Our new school (built out of locally harvested bamboo) is gorgeous and bustling with more than two hundred and thirty children from Surkhet and surrounding regions. Many of our students are the first in their families to attend school.

The children are thriving. I truly believe that if all the children in the world are provided with their most basic needs and rights—a safe home, medical care, an education, and love—they will grow up to be leaders and end the cycles of poverty and violence in our world.

Anything is possible. I know that no matter how many times people tell you that, you really can't hear it enough. Maybe it's a cliché because it's *true*. You can do anything you put your mind to, and you just have to do it.

I've learned this lesson again and again, mostly from watching my children. They have overcome some of the most unbelievable suffering—sorrow beyond measure. I watch them—their bright eyes, their incredible resilience, the way they get up and keep on going, the way they know, somewhere deep in their hearts, that the only way is to keep moving onward and to keep loving. If love is still possible after you've lost everything you've ever known, then anything is possible. That's what I think.

Anything is possible.

I'm telling you there's a lot to do. I'm telling you the world needs you. Whatever your calling is. Whatever you dream of. The world needs all of us. I'm telling you. Everything you need, you've got right now. So go.

One step at a time.

The world will cheer you on. Trust me.

Mitch Albom

Bestselling Author, Journalist, and Philanthropist

Giving Is Living

Morrie was dying. We came to sit by his side. Family. Friends. Former students.

Not everyone was so comfortable. Death can make you squeamish. Many visitors, I noticed, came with a plan. They were going to tell happy stories, share jokes, show photos. They'd go into Morrie's office, where he lay motionless in a long chair. The door would shut. And an hour later they'd emerge in tears.

But they were crying about . . . *their* job, *their* divorce, *their* issues.

"I went in to cheer him up," they'd say, sniffing, "but he started asking me about my life and my problems and, next thing I know, I was bawling."

I watched this happen so many times that finally I went in to Morrie and said, "I don't get it. You're the one dying from ALS, this awful, debilitating disease. If ever anyone has finally earned the right to say, 'Let's not talk about your problems, let's talk about my problems,' it's you!"

He looked at me sadly.

"Mitch," he whispered, "why would I ever *take* like that? Taking just reminds me that I'm dying." He smiled. "Giving makes me feel like I'm living."

Giving makes me feel like I'm living.

It is a profound little sentence.

And some of the best advice I've ever received.

Our culture, of course, tells us the opposite. The more you take, the more alive you are. The more money in your bank account, cars in your garage, or shoes in your closet, the more you are winning the game.

But think about your final moments in this world, like the ones Morrie endured. At that most crucial time, when you are clinging to life, all that you own will be of no use to you. What purpose will a sports car serve at that point? Jewelry? A big-screen TV? Chances are that stuff won't even be in the room.

All that will matter, at that precious point, is that the people who love you are by your side, right? Well, the people who love you will likely be the ones to whom you gave time. The ones to whom you gave warmth and affection. When you most want to feel alive, the things you gave will be the things that return.

Try it sometime—maybe the next time you're depressed or blue. Maybe the next time taking something or achieving status doesn't make you as happy as you thought it would. Instead, go someplace where you're needed—talk to a struggling friend, cheer up someone in a hospital, scoop potatoes at a soup kitchen. You'll be surprised how energized you feel afterward, how your blues may quietly disappear when you see someone who has it worse.

And if, on your way out, you get that small tingle in your stomach when those people whisper "Thank you"?

That's being alive.

And it comes from giving, not taking.

Morrie, once again, had it right.

Michael J. Fox
Actor, Bestselling Author, and Activist

___

Be Grateful

As much as we can, it's helpful to be in a place of gratitude. None of us is entitled to anything. We get what we get not because we want it or we deserve it or because it's unfair if we don't get it but because we earn it, we respect it, and only if we share it do we keep it.

Scott Case

Technologist, Inventor, Co-Founder of Priceline.com, Vice Chairman
of Malaria No More, and CEO of Startup America Partnership

You're Sitting on a Winning Lottery Ticket—
Invest It Wisely

When I graduated from college in 1992, I felt as if I had hit the lottery. Not the actual lottery—I'm not talking about Ferraris or private yachts—but the life lottery. First, I live in America, a country where you can reach any goal you set for yourself, as long as you've got the guts to work for it. Second, I had received an education. Literacy alone opens doors that people all over the world can only dream of. Third, I knew that I had a support system behind me; the love of my family had gotten me this far, and now it was time to put my prize to use.

After college, I parlayed my lottery ticket into a career at the beginning of the Internet era. I was lucky enough to belong to a team that worked to design, build, and grow an innovative business called Priceline.com. I then went on to grow a Web service called Network for Good, which has helped sixty thousand nonprofits raise more than $400 million online.

Most recently, I've directed my energy toward doing whatever I can to stop mosquitoes from needlessly killing hundreds of thousands of kids every year. I lead a team at Malaria No More, which is dedicated to one thing: ending malaria deaths in Africa by 2015.

The chance to work every day to have a positive effect on other people is the chance of a lifetime. I believe that everyone has the same opportunity—and it comes with a daunting responsibility. It won't always be easy. It won't always be fun. But it will be rewarding.

So don't take your own winning lottery ticket for granted. Invest the skills, knowledge, and talents that come with it to make the world a better place through science or technology, academia or advocacy, or community or public service.

Your winning lottery ticket doesn't get more valuable by sitting on it—invest it in a better future for all of us.

William J. Clinton

Forty-second President of the United States, Founder of the
Clinton Global Initiative and the William J. Clinton Foundation

---

Be a Good Citizen

When I graduated from college in 1968, the definition of being a good citizen was to get as much education as you could; work hard for the money you're paid; be a responsible parent and neighbor; obey the law and pay your taxes; and cast an informed vote at election time.

But today's world is more diverse and interdependent than ever before, and for this reason, there is another item to add to the list: You also have to do what you can as private citizens to tackle our common problems and advance the public good.

No matter how good government policies are or how much economic growth we enjoy, there is always going to be a gap between what the private sector can produce and what the government can provide. In that space, citizens have to take action to bridge the broken places in our society and around the world.

This idea is slightly older than the United States. Benjamin Franklin organized the first volunteer Fire Department in Philadelphia before the U.S. Constitution was ratified. Today, we have a million nongovernmental organizations in America, and more than 350,000 religious organizations working to heal the broken places in society.

You are carrying the future of America in your heart and your mind. So live your dreams and remember, whatever you choose to do with your life, you must also be a citizen of your country, your nation, and our interdependent world. Because while our differences make life more fascinating, our common humanity matters more.

PART 9

WHAT BOATS ARE BUILT FOR

On Taking Risks and Seeking Opportunity

Only those who dare to fail can ever achieve greatly.
—ROBERT F. KENNEDY

I loved working on the *Today* show. The hours stunk, but I had even come to love mornings in Manhattan. The rosy gray hues at sunrise, the shiny, hosed-down sidewalks, the determined, solitary runners that few are up and about to see. But after fifteen years I was worried, not that the show had become stale but that I would become stale doing it. So when CBS, specifically Les Moonves, began wooing me to come anchor its evening newscast I was flattered and intrigued. And I felt that I had a unique opportunity to show that a female could have this high-profile position and own it. I wanted young girls to watch and dream just a bit bigger.

Someone recently put a pinprick in this lofty and perhaps self-important notion. I met a woman on vacation who told me that on the night of my first broadcast she picked up her daughter (who must have been about seven at the time) from school and told her they were going to watch the *Evening News* together because this was a big day for women. As she recounted this important mother-daughter moment, I was filled with pride. "We watched that night," she told me. "And we never watched you again." Realizing that she might have insulted me, she added sheepishly, "We don't really watch TV."

But leaving a successful morning show and my colleagues, especially Matt, was daunting. So I convened my kitchen cabinet (i.e., my two daughters, Ellie and Carrie) around the kitchen table and asked them what they thought. Ellie told me to go for it, and thought a change would do me good. Carrie, who was ten, said, "Mommy, you'll be the first woman to do this job by yourself. You have to do it!" Without encouragement from my daughters, my parents, and a trusted circle of friends, I'm not sure I would have made the leap. But I'll never forget the note that a producer from the *Today* show wrote me shortly after I announced I was making the move. "A boat is always safe in the harbor," she wrote. "But that's not what boats are built for."

Going to CBS has taught me that getting out of your comfort zone is, well, uncomfortable. But as Mark Twain once wrote, "Twenty years from now you will be more disappointed by the things you didn't do than by the ones you did do." I know I would have regretted not seizing this opportunity for the rest of my life.

So get out of the harbor. The territory may be uncharted and the water may get pretty choppy at times, but you'll be amazed at what you learn, especially about yourself. And, through it all, make sure you have a handful of people you can always depend on to throw you a life preserver when things get really rough.

Ellen DeGeneres

Stand-up Comedian and Emmy Award–Winning Talk-Show Host

——

Be True to Yourself

When I finished school, I was completely lost. And by school I mean middle school, but I went ahead and finished high school anyway. I really had no ambition—I didn't know what I wanted to do. I did everything. I shucked oysters, I was a hostess, I was a bartender, I was a waitress, I painted houses, I sold vacuum cleaners—I had no idea. And I thought I'd just finally settle in some job and I would make enough money to pay my rent, maybe have basic cable, maybe not. I didn't really have a plan. My point is that by the time I was entering adulthood I really thought I knew who I was, but I had no idea. Like for example, when I was twenty I was dating men. So what I'm saying is, when you're older most of you will be gay.

Anyway, I had no idea what I wanted to do with my life, and the way I ended up on this path was from a very tragic event. I was maybe nineteen, and my girlfriend at the time was killed in a car accident. And I passed the accident and I didn't know it was her and I kept going, and I found out shortly after that it was her. And I was living in a basement apartment, I had no money, I had no heat, no air; I had a mattress on the floor and the apartment was infested with fleas. And I was soul-searching. I was like, Why is she suddenly gone and there are fleas here? I don't understand, there must be a purpose, and wouldn't it be so convenient if we could pick up the phone and call God and ask these questions.

I started writing, and what poured out of me was an imaginary conversation with God, which was one-sided, and I finished writing it and I looked at it and I said to myself—and I had never done stand-up, ever, there was no club in town—I said, "I'm gonna do this on *The Tonight Show* with Johnny Carson"—at the time he was the king—"and I'm gonna be the first woman in the history of the show to be called over to sit down." And, several years later, I was the first woman in the history of the show, and the only woman in the history of the show to sit down, because of that phone conversation with God that I wrote. And I started this path of stand-up, and it was successful and it was great, but it was hard, because I was trying to please everybody and I had this secret that I was keeping: that I was gay. I thought that if people found out they wouldn't like me, they wouldn't laugh at me.

Then my career really took off. In 1994, I got my own sitcom, *Ellen,* and reached another level of success. And I thought, What if they find out I'm gay, then they'll never watch (this was a long time ago, this was when we just had white presidents—this was back many years ago). And I finally decided that I was living with so much shame, and so much fear, that I just couldn't live that way anymore, and I decided to come out and make it creative. My character would come out at the same time, and it wasn't to make a political statement; it wasn't to do anything other than free myself up from this heaviness that I was carrying around. I just wanted to be honest. And I thought, What's the worst that could happen? I could lose my career. Well, I did. I lost my career.

The network canceled the show after six years, without even telling me; I read it in the paper. The phone didn't ring for three years. I had no offers. Nobody wanted to touch me at all. Yet I was getting letters from kids who almost committed suicide, but didn't, because of what I did. And I realized that I had a purpose. And it wasn't just about me, and it wasn't about celebrity. But I still felt that I was being punished. It was a bad time—I was angry, I was sad—and then I was offered a talk show. And the people who offered me the talk show tried to sell it. Most stations didn't want to pick it up. Most people didn't want to buy it because they thought nobody would watch me.

Today, *The Ellen DeGeneres Show* is in its eighth season and has won thirty-one Daytime Emmy Awards. Really, when I look back on it I wouldn't change a thing. I mean, it was so important for me to lose everything, because I found out what the most important thing is: to be true to yourself. Ultimately, that's what's gotten me to this place. I don't live in fear—I'm free, I have no secrets, and I know I'll always be okay, because no matter what, I know who I am.

So, in conclusion, when I was younger I thought success was something different. I thought, When I grow up I want to be famous. I want to be a star. I want to be in movies. When I grow up, I want to see the world, drive nice cars, I want to have groupies. To quote the Pussycat Dolls. How many people thought it was "boobies," by the way? It's not—it's "groupies."

The definition of success changes throughout your life. For me, the most important thing is to live with integrity, and not to give in to peer pressure. Never try to be something that you're not. To live your life as an honest and compassionate person. Those are the most important qualities to me. Stay true to yourself. Never follow anyone else's path, unless you're in the woods and you're lost and you see a path; then, by all means, you should follow that path. And don't give advice; it will come back and bite you in the ass. Don't take anyone's advice, either. So my advice to you is to be true to yourself and everything will be fine.

Condoleezza Rice

Sixty-sixth Secretary of State of the United States
and Stanford University Professor

Find Your Next Adventure

As I traveled the world representing the United States as our nation's sixty-sixth secretary of state, I was often asked how I overcame the struggles of segregation in the Deep South and developed an interest in the Soviet Union at a time when few blacks—let alone women—were expected to pursue a career in international politics. I would reply, "I started as a failed piano major."

In all seriousness, my story was possible only through the blessings of my parents, who provided me with a supportive, nurturing environment of family, faith, and community. They believed firmly in the transformative power of education and were committed, despite their modest means, to providing me with anything that could be called an educational opportunity. They also gave me a piece of advice that helped me overcome the horrors of racism in segregated Birmingham: They reminded me that even if I could not control my circumstances, I could control my response to them.

My parents gave me another gift as well: the freedom to try and, on occasion, to fail. Throughout my youth, they encouraged me to try anything new and challenging without worrying about whether I would be a success. I spent the bulk of my teenage years figure skating, and although I wasn't very good, I worked hard and eventually developed the kind of commitment and discipline that I draw upon to this day. I had also been convinced from an early age that I was going to be a concert pianist. It wasn't until I wandered into a class on international politics during college, taught by Josef Korbel, Madeleine Albright's father, that I discovered my passion for foreign affairs.

The point is that life is full of surprises and serendipity. Being open to unexpected turns in the road is an important part of success. If you try to plan every step, you may miss those wonderful twists and turns. Just find your next adventure—do it well, enjoy it—and then, not now, think about what comes next.

Matt Lauer

Journalist and Host of the *Today* show

———

Sometimes You Gotta Go Off Course

Sometimes you get a piece of advice that just sounds all wrong! It seems to go against everything you've been taught, and takes you far outside your comfort zone. Following advice like that can be scary and unsettling, but that doesn't mean you should ignore it. In fact, unconventional advice can force you to examine a situation from another angle and give you perspective that you might not have found on your own.

While I was a senior at Ohio University, I was offered an internship at a small television station in Huntington, West Virginia. I wouldn't be paid a salary, but in exchange for spending ten weeks living in Huntington I would get a few credits and a lot of real-world experience. There was one big issue, however. Accepting the internship would cause me to miss a couple of courses that were required in order to graduate with the rest of my class that spring! I simply couldn't do both. It was either the internship and the hands-on learning that came with it or the required courses and the completion of my degree, on schedule, with the friends I had spent four years with at O.U.

Every bone in my body told me to stay on campus, take the courses, and graduate on time. I've always been prompt (almost to a fault). I'm the guy who arrives fifteen minutes early for appointments and organizes his day down to the second. Being late for anything makes me crazy! The thought of graduating late was hard to imagine.

I decided to run the situation by my father before making a final decision. My father started his career as an insurance salesman before changing fields and getting into the bicycle business. He knew almost nothing about the television industry. Even though he did not have experience in my chosen field, he had a wealth of common sense. He was practical (not a shocking trait for a former insurance salesman) and conservative in his approach to life and business. I assumed that he would tell me to follow the safe course and get my diploma on time.

But after some thought my father told me that he truly believed I should take the internship in West Virginia. He said that while graduating was something we both felt was important, the exact date of the event itself was fairly meaningless. He saw the internship as a chance to learn things that textbooks couldn't teach me—an adventure that I shouldn't pass up.

I took a deep breath and followed my dad's advice.

He couldn't have known how valuable his guidance would prove to be. I completed my internship in West Virginia and was asked to become a producer of the station's newscast as soon as the spring quarter ended. I took that job and never looked back, moving from one city to the next and from each job on to something bigger and better! Had I stayed in school and passed on that internship, I would have finished on time only *then* to begin my job search along with every other graduate of 1979. Instead, I had a job in hand and a valuable head start!

Oh, by the way, I did get that diploma—eighteen years later, on the day that I gave the commencement address at O.U.! As my father said, the date of the event was fairly meaningless!

General David H. Petraeus

Commander of the NATO International Security Assistance Force
and U.S. Forces–Afghanistan

Be Comfortable with the Uncomfortable

Our nation's twenty-sixth president, Theodore Roosevelt, once observed, "Far and away the best prize that life has to offer is the chance to work hard at work worth doing." During the course of my thirty-six years in uniform, I have found great truth in that statement. Nothing beats the satisfaction of knowing that the work into which you pour time, energy, and talent is meaningful.

Meaningful work can, of course, take many forms. Mine—like that of hundreds of thousands of other Americans in uniform—has taken the form of military service. But any endeavor that reaches beyond self and contributes to the greater good is "work worth doing."

As TR knew—and as those of us in uniform have discovered on numerous occasions, in recent years in particular—work worth doing is often hard work. And one of the best ways I've found to prepare for the hard work of meaningful work is to pursue experiences that take me out of my intellectual comfort zone. I owe that life lesson to the great General Jack Galvin, a lifelong mentor and friend for whom I worked on multiple occasions when I was a captain and then a major. During one of my tours with him, as I was weighing options for my next assignment, General Galvin advised me that I should eschew another typical infantry assignment and instead pursue an "out of my intellectual comfort zone" experience by going to graduate school. That ranked with the best advice I ever received.

At Princeton University's Woodrow Wilson School, where I was privileged to study, I was forced out of the relatively cloistered, nose-to-the-grindstone existence that we in the military tend to live. Not only did I gain a healthy degree of intellectual humility, I also came to realize that "not all of these smart folks think the same way I do." Those and other experiences in graduate school—and others in similar endeavors over the years—helped stretch my mind and my imagination, challenged my ways of thinking, and, I'd like to think, developed in me a degree of intellectual flexibility and creativity. Indeed, my experience at Princeton is one of the reasons I advise today's young military leaders to go to graduate school, to immerse themselves in foreign cultures, and, in essence, to do "off-the-wall" stuff. We all benefit from learning to be comfortable with the uncomfortable.

Indeed, being comfortable outside my comfort zone—and believing in the value of the work those of us in uniform pursue—has helped enable me at various points in my career to take on tasks that some have considered "mission impossible." Being comfortable with the uncomfortable helped me in the early days in Iraq, when I realized that, contrary to pre-operation expectations, we were going to engage in nation-building as well as conventional military operations. Being comfortable with the uncomfortable also helped prepare me to sit before congressional committees amid intense focus and scrutiny over our missions in Iraq and Afghanistan, to testify to those missions being "hard but not hopeless," and to accept responsibility for leading our remarkable troopers in undertaking those missions. Indeed, I often counsel young leaders not to be afraid of taking on an exceedingly difficult task—so long as the task is "work worth doing" and they are prepared to be uncomfortable as they work hard at it.

Fareed Zakaria

International Affairs Journalist and Bestselling Author

Run Fast, but Don't Run Scared

My best advice takes off from Franklin Roosevelt's famous quotation "The only thing we have to fear is fear itself." The most important thing to remember for a person coming out of school, or looking around for a new job, or dealing with the pressures of life, is not to get scared—to view all of these transitional moments as opportunities, not as threats. Americans do their best when they view the world as full of boundless opportunities and challenges.

The phrase "can do" is an American phrase. No other country has this idea as part of its daily discourse. Having a "can do" personality or a "can do" attitude really says something intrinsic about Americans. They look at the world and see problems to be solved, not problems to be managed, not problems to be endured. We are not a fatalistic country. I think that one of the key personal attributes that will help anyone, anywhere, is the ability to "look on the bright side." This might sound mawkish, but actually it's a very profound insight into how you should look at the world. Believe that you can succeed and thrive and prosper and you will find the opportunities that will allow you to do so. You will find the glasses that are half full. You will discover that the things that look like obstacles are really ladders on the way to advancement.

I came to America from Bombay in 1982, a time when India was among the twenty poorest countries in the world. I was a scholarship kid at Yale, and I had no contacts and no money. I came from a nice middle-class family in India, with educated parents, so I had enormous advantages, but it was also a bit overwhelming to come to a place where I knew nobody and was totally on my own. And America, by the way, was in the midst of what was being called the worst recession since the Great Depression, the recession of the early 1980s. In addition, Americans were still dealing with the aftermath of Vietnam and Watergate. It easily could have seemed like a time of despair, but to me it didn't. Maybe it was just naïveté and being young, but I saw boundless opportunities and I set out to find ways to use every one of them.

My father was a very driven man, always looking for ways to move ahead, and that probably has had a big impact on my life. But being in America really made the difference for me. There weren't any prizes being offered to me on a platter, but there were opportunities. There were also challenges. I was in a new country—an unfamiliar culture with no contacts and little money. I didn't see the obstacles as much, though, because I was intrigued by the opportunities. None of the challenges I faced seemed very scary to me; they didn't get me down. The danger, in being frightened or dispirited, is that you begin to view the world you're in as one that is dangerous and threatening and you try to blame somebody else for your problems. I never for a moment thought there was any racism or double standard being applied to me because I was an Indian, or a foreign student, or because I didn't have fancy clothes. I never looked for any of that. I was busy looking for opportunities, not trying to find explanations for why things weren't perfect. I found America to be incredibly open and accepting, and I really never experienced any type of discrimination. I certainly knew people at the time who had a different experience, and I think some of it was reality. But sometimes you find what you search for. I wanted to define my life by what I was able to do, not by what I was unable to do.

I look at America today, and perhaps the greatest danger we face is that we're in a completely new world—a world that no American has ever had to deal with before—in which everyone is part of a global economic system. People everywhere are playing by our rules—free trade, free markets, free enterprise—and they're playing to win. We should be delighted, because it means a bigger world, a richer world, a world where more people are escaping poverty and more people are able to pursue the American dream. But many Americans are fearful of what this might mean. *We might not be on top. Workers from other countries are stealing our jobs.* When you start getting into the fear business, you blame your problems on other people. But if other people are doing well, it's not because they're cheating. It's because they're working hard—they're going to school, they're excelling in math and science. Fear and blame are essentially pointless. You can't stop China from growing. What you *can* do is figure out how to succeed in this new world—there are a hundred different ways—and Americans are well positioned to do so.

The hand the United States has been dealt remains the best compared with all others. This is a country with enormous potential, great human talent, the best companies in the world, the best universities in the world, an amazing geographical position where it can access both the Asian world and the European world. But Americans have gotten themselves down and have lost faith in themselves and are now blaming other people for their problems. If you listen to the political discourse in America today, you would think that all our problems have been caused by the Mexicans or the Chinese or the Muslims. The reality is that we have caused our own problems. Whatever has happened has been caused by isolating ourselves or blaming others.

More important, we're not going to succeed by trying to be like someone else. We can succeed only by trying to be more like us. That is, an open, dynamic, competitive society and economy. The further away we get from a sense of openness and tolerance of differences and diversity, the more we betray American ideals and the uniquely American attitude in the world. So I would say that my best advice for these times is: Don't let fear guide how you think about the world. Run fast, but don't run scared.

Indra Nooyi

CEO of PepsiCo

Opportunity Will Find You

There really is nothing like a concrete "life plan" to weigh you down. Because if you always have one eye on some future goal, you stop paying attention to the job at hand, miss opportunities that might arise, and stay fixedly on one path even when a better, newer course might have opened up.

When I was growing up in Chennai, India, I had no idea that I would one day be the head of PepsiCo. I majored in chemistry at university. My heroes were people like Paul Berg, who shared a Nobel Prize in Chemistry for his work on DNA. I wasn't looking to go into big business. I had no dreams of being a CEO. I just did every job I had to the best of my ability, and the opportunities found me.

Being able to change course is more important today than ever. The world is in flux—technologically, socially, and economically—but it's also increasingly interconnected. This means that we have many more opportunities before us than preceding generations ever had. You can work anywhere in the world, and choose an infinite number of roles and careers. In this rapidly changing environment, not knowing where your path will take you is no cause for panic. In fact, it gives you a competitive edge. It leaves you open to change, adaptation, and opportunities. *It's a wonderful, enviable position to be in.*

In some ways, we are all like the great explorers from history. Faced with an ocean of opportunities and uncertainties, people like Christopher Columbus set out without a proper map but with great determination to make their mark on the world. Columbus thought that he would find India. Okay, so he found America instead—and opened up incredible opportunities for all of us. If you remain open to new opportunities and intellectual growth, you will *always* be on the right path, even if you don't reach the destination you expected.

Jane Lynch

Emmy Award–Winning Actress and Comedian

———

Life Is a Series of Happy Accidents

Relax. Really. Just relax. Don't sweat it. For a long time, I was so anxious and fearful that the parade would pass me by. I was sure that someone or something outside myself had all the answers. I was driven by an anxiety-filled ambition. I wanted to be a working actor so badly. Today, I am a working actor, and I guarantee you it's not because I suffered or worried over it. As I look back, the road my life has taken has been a series of happy accidents, and I was either smart or stupid enough to take advantage of them. I thought I had to have a plan, a strategy. Turns out I just had to be ready and willing to take chances, to look at what was right in front of me, and to put my whole heart into everything I pursued. Anxiety and fear did not help or fuel anything. Sometimes you just have to learn to get out of your own way. I know there are a lot of folks out there who are hoping for some words of wisdom or keys to the kingdom or that I might let them in on the Big Secret. So I will defer to Carol Brady, who in her infinite wisdom once said, "Find out what you do best and do your best with it."

Marissa Mayer

Vice-President of Consumer Products at Google

When There Isn't a Right Choice . . .

I graduated from Stanford University in 1999, with a master's degree in computer science. It was the height of the Internet bubble, and I had fourteen job offers lined up. Yes, it was that long ago. I usually like having choices, but this was ridiculous! I couldn't make up my mind.

One evening, my friend André, an economist, helped me weigh all fourteen options. Being a computer scientist, I love logic and data, so I created a big matrix: one row for each job, with columns for salary, location, quality of life, career trajectory, and likely happiness, all rated on a scale from one to ten. André and I drew up charts, graphs, and equations, and it was all so incredibly focused and detailed and analytical that by midnight I just totally lost it and collapsed into tears.

André would have none of it. He just stopped and said, "You know, Marissa, you're putting so much pressure on yourself to make the right choice. You're approaching this as if there's one right answer. And I have to be honest, that's just not what I'm seeing here." He gestured toward the matrices and charts strewn across the floor. "I think you have a bunch of good options, and then there's the one that you'll pick and make great."

I went to bed and slept on it. When I woke up the next morning, I just knew that I had to work for this twelve-person start-up with a goofy name: Google. I wanted to join Google because I felt that the smartest people were working there, because in many ways I felt utterly unprepared for it, and for a whole host of other reasons that I could barely articulate. In the end, I couldn't have made a better choice.

André's insight that night taught me an important lesson: misperceiving that there is one correct choice is a common mistake. Coming to understand that there are usually a few good choices—and then there's the one you pick, commit to, and make great—is the best way to make flexible, optimal, good decisions in life.

Eric Schmidt

Executive Chairman of Google

Say Yes

Find a way to say yes to things. Say yes to invitations to a new country, say yes to meet new friends, say yes to learn something new. Yes is how you get your first job, and your next job, and your spouse, and even your kids. Even if it's a bit edgy, a bit out of your comfort zone, saying yes means that you will do something new, meet someone new, and make a difference. Yes lets you stand out in a crowd, be the optimist, see the glass full, be the one everyone comes to. Yes is what keeps us all young.

Maya Angelou

Poet, Educator, Historian, and Bestselling Author

———

Make Your Own Path

My paternal grandmother, Mrs. Annie Henderson, gave me advice that I have used for sixty-five years. She said, "If the world puts you on a road you do not like, if you look ahead and do not want that destination which is being offered and you look behind and you do not want to return to your place of departure, step off the road. Build yourself a brand-new path."

Ruth J. Simmons
President of Brown University

—

A Cold Bucket of Water

Aaron Lemonick and I were worlds apart in many respects. He was a physicist and I am a humanist. He was white and I am black. He was Jewish and I am Baptist. But through these differences we forged the closest of friendships. He played a decisive role in my life and helped me make one of the biggest leaps of my career.

Aaron Lemonick was the dean of the faculty at Princeton when he persuaded me to become his associate dean. Our partnership was a close one from the very first moment. That isn't to say that we always agreed; our experiences were different enough that our perspectives on issues sometimes collided. In spite of that, I had enormous respect for him because of his honesty, his warmth, and his courage. I'd had a very successful career at Princeton when, ten years into my tenure there, I was approached about the presidency of Smith College, an all-women's college in Northampton, Massachusetts. Although I was at first reluctant to be considered, I eventually agreed to an interview, knowing that in the end I might well decline an offer.

There were many reasons for my uncertainty and skepticism. From what I knew of the demanding nature of presidencies, I was not at all sure that the position fit my personality. As vice-provost, I rather liked the freedom that I enjoyed to identify problems and advocate for solutions without having to be responsible to a wide range of constituents. Furthermore, still identifying as an outsider in the academy, I was skeptical about whether I could credibly embody an institution as its president. Despite these concerns, I was offered the Smith presidency.

I sought guidance from friends and colleagues as to whether I should accept the position. For the most part, those at Princeton argued against my doing so. They offered a variety of reasons: the work in which I was involved at Princeton was at a critical point; Smith, while a major liberal-arts college, was "only" a women's college; there would be many other offers and I should wait for one that was ideal for me, etc. A few, however, suggested that this was a wonderful opportunity and that I would be able to adapt to the Smith environment and, in time, grow more comfortable in a leadership role.

Fortunately, Aaron Lemonick took me out to lunch to discuss the Smith offer. Although I no longer worked for him at the time, he remained my most trusted adviser and my greatest advocate. That day in the Annex Restaurant on Nassau Street, across from the Princeton campus, we sat and talked about Smith and my future. At the end of a lengthy exchange, he asked, "Ruth, what could possibly prevent you from accepting the Smith presidency?" In response, I echoed much of what others had told me: it might be the wrong time, I had unfinished work at Princeton; I wasn't sure that I wanted to be a president anyway, and so on. Aaron listened patiently before saying, "Ruth, Princeton has been here for two hundred and fifty years. If you leave, you will hardly be missed at all."

His comment, like a cold bucket of water thrown into my face, revealed clearly how absurd it was to use the importance of my work at Princeton as a reason to turn down an offer to be the president of a leading college. If I was to turn it down, I needed to confront the real reasons for my reluctance. I asked Aaron what he thought of the admonition that other offers would come along at a more opportune time. He told me unblinkingly that no such guarantee existed. Finally, he allayed my concerns about whether I was ready, pointing out that I would no doubt make mistakes but that he had every confidence that I had the temperament and the intelligence to succeed.

Aaron's advice broke the logjam and exposed my fear of being tested as Smith's president. Throughout my years in the academy, I had worked to overcome feelings of inadequacy—feelings that many of my generation who began their education in segregated schools shared. To find myself leading a so-called élite college was a great leap from how my education had begun in a small colored school in Grapeland, Texas.

Aaron's advice enabled me to focus on what leading Smith could mean for me and, more important, what it could mean for others like me. The risk was unmistakably plain, but the possibility of crossing such a barrier, I recognized, would have great personal meaning and satisfaction. I thought about my parents, the limited opportunities that had been open to them in the South, and the satisfaction they would have had to see me become president of Smith. I thought about the students whom I always encouraged to overcome self-doubt and barriers to achievement and wondered how I could fail to do what I asked of them. The path seemed clearer.

I accepted the Smith presidency and spent six satisfying years there before becoming the president of Brown University. Aaron was present at each of my presidential inaugurations, smiling proudly and no doubt feeling a measure of satisfaction that he had managed to bring me to my senses.

Stephen Colbert

Bestselling Author, Satirist, and Host of *The Colbert Report*

Yes . . . and That's the Word

Say yes to any opportunity to do anything even close to what you dream of doing. This will sometimes get you in over your head, but that will just make you swim harder. It's the best way to meet other people who love to do what you love to do. You will learn from and comfort each other.

Steve Martin
Award-Winning Actor, Comedian, Author, and Playwright

Take Chances

I have always remembered this line from e. e. cummings's "Six Nonlec-tures." It motivated me to take chances with my craft and my life. I think it's more relevant for a young person than for an older person, and I put it in the category of inspiration rather than advice: "Who would be 'secure'? Every and any slave."

PART 10

FIND THE JOY

On Wisdom and Happiness

Each morning when I open my eyes I say to myself: I, not events, have the power to make me happy or unhappy today. I can choose which it shall be. Yesterday is dead, tomorrow hasn't arrived yet. I have just one day, today, and I'm going to be happy in it.

—GROUCHO MARX

When I was a desk assistant at ABC News in Washington, I idolized a correspondent named Cassie Mackin. She had been a reporter for the Baltimore *Sun* and was ABC's most glamorous correspondent: blond, willowy, and oh-so-chic. I watched in awe as she seemed to float through the newsroom. Cassie Mackin died of cancer when she was forty-two. Her funeral was televised, and I looked at the pallbearers. There were people like Ted Kennedy and a cameraman named Rolfe Tessem, professional colleagues. Cassie had never married and had no children. Suddenly, at age twenty-six, I found my die-hard career ambitions shifting. I didn't want this to happen to me. I wanted a husband, a family. I did not want my job to be my life. It was a real wake-up call.

I did marry and have children. But after Jay died life as I knew it vanished. I was inundated with books about grief, from C. S. Lewis to Elisabeth Kübler-Ross. I read them all. But then I came across a quote by Thomas Jefferson that helped me recalibrate and get my bearings. It was simple but profound, and almost harsh in its directness: "The earth belongs to the living, not the dead." I think about and miss Jay every single day, especially during those parent-child rites of passage, like recitals and graduations. But I realized that we all have a finite amount of time on this planet. We are all terminal. And, whether our lives are long or cut tragically short, while we're here we have an obligation to find and give joy—in the beauty of our surroundings, in the pleasure of the moment, and in the company of those we love. It's been said over and over that no one on his deathbed ever says, "Gee, I wish I had spent more time at the office." Once, when Jay was so very sick, he turned to me and said, "You know, nothing really matters except your friends and family." We are often so busy running as fast as we can on that hamster wheel of success, we often don't take time to appreciate each other, to nurture and tend to our relationships with the people we love. So now I try to savor every moment, and am awed without embarrassment by a water-colored sunset or the tininess of a baby's foot. I cherish talking about everything and nothing with my parents in our family den that I remember so well, surrounded by my father's beautiful books, or laughing uncontrollably with my daughters over something silly. Anna Quindlen, one of my favorite writers and people, perhaps put it best in her book *A Short Guide to a Happy Life:* "Life is made up of moments, small pieces of glittering mica in a long stretch of gray cement. It would be wonderful if they would come to us unsummoned, but particularly in lives as busy as the ones most of us lead now, that won't happen. We have to teach ourselves how to make room for them, to love them, and to live, really live." In other words, find the joy.

Jimmy Kimmel

Late-Night Television Host and Comedian

Wisdom You Can Eat

My family isn't the type that gives advice. My family gives headaches. Whenever I hear others recount the best advice their parents ever gave them, I wonder what I missed. Why didn't my father call me into his study, with pipe in hand and newspaper folded neatly over his knee, to give me the kind of simple but poetic life advice that fathers like Mr. Cunningham and Sheriff Andy Taylor gave Ron Howard? Maybe it was because my dad didn't have a study. Maybe he was too busy. Maybe it was racism of the most unusual sort.

On the day I left Las Vegas for college in Arizona, I stopped at my aunt and uncle's house to say goodbye. As I backed out of their driveway, my Uncle Frank suddenly bolted toward my car. I stopped, rolled the window down, and heard him say, "Remember, Jim. Safety first." I paused, agreed to put safety first, and then, as I pulled away, ran over his foot.

My Aunt Chippy sometimes shares her thoughts with others, but I'm not sure you'd call it advice. Some of my favorite nuggets are: "Put some clothes on—you look like a whore!" and "Let's not make a whole schkabutz about this!" Don't bother googling it. *Schkabutz* isn't a word. But we knew what she meant.

The best and only real advice my father ever gave me came on a dreaded family road trip. My dad didn't like to waste money on extravagances like FM radio and transmission fluid, and so our sixteen-year-old Chevy Impala station wagon, as dictated by tradition, broke down halfway to Knott's Berry Farm. There was no fast food within sight of the gas station, which meant that my parents were forced to take us to a restaurant that employed something called a "waitress." The diner was filthy and the food scared us. As we scoured the menu, my father gifted me with a pearl of wisdom that I have since shared with my children. He said, "When in doubt, order the hamburger."

Not exactly Sophocles, but I did order the hamburger and, when in doubt, I still do.

Jane Aronson, M.D.

Founder of the Worldwide Orphans Foundation

Dare to Be Happy

I achieved my lifelong dream in 1986, when I graduated from medical school at the age of thirty-five. But there was another dream, a secret, which I rarely discussed with anyone: to have a family. To be a mother. I had come out as a gay woman in 1971 at the age of nineteen, and this life choice seemed to require that I become a "professional woman." It wasn't that I saw myself as an old maid, but somehow I knew that I should define myself chiefly by work. So I worked very hard, spent eighty hours a week taking care of children with unusual infections, including HIV/AIDS, and orphans adopted from abroad. In the meantime, I found a life partner and developed a sweet circle of good friends. I was busy traveling, growing a pediatric specialty in adoption medicine, and I created a foundation to improve the lives of orphans around the world. What could be more fulfilling?

But still I yearned for a child. I often cried in the restroom at work after seeing yet another deliriously joyful couple walk into my examining room with an adorable baby adopted from Vietnam, China, or Cambodia. I imagined myself as a parent and often spent hours reading *The New York Times* at the local playground, just so that I could watch children play in the sandbox and run to their moms and dads when a friend grabbed their shovel. I befriended many adoptive parents and became involved in their families. But I was convinced that I would never have what they had.

The pain grew to be an issue in my relationship, because my partner didn't want to have any more children; she already had two who were grown and didn't want to start over. But my sadness and yearning wouldn't go away.

I struggled with the idea of having children for another reason, too: self-doubt. Would I even be a good mother? Did I know how? I'd had a challenging upbringing, with little nurturing from my own mother. I feared that I would be the same kind of parent she'd been: distant and unavailable. I felt stuck in this bind—whether to break up a long-term relationship to have children by myself, whether to risk losing love and never finding it again, whether to chance the discovery that I'd actually be a bad parent, too.

So I shelved the fantasy for decades, paralyzed by indecision, anxiety, and disappointment.

Then one night I went to dinner with a new acquaintance, the parent of a newly adopted Chinese baby girl. This woman was a dynamic business executive who had adopted a baby at a mature age. Somewhere during dinner, after we discussed her daughter, her business, and my dreams for my ongoing work with orphans around the world, she looked across the table and asked, "Why don't you have children?" I answered quickly and definitively, without any connection to the truth: "I take care of other people's children." She just as swiftly replied, "That's ridiculous. You want children, don't you?" And suddenly I found myself being honest with a stranger, like what happens on an airplane when one starts pouring out secrets to an arbitrary seatmate. I revealed the conflicts I had, my fears that I would not be a loving mother, the reality that my partner didn't want children.

My new friend gave me some advice that changed everything. "You should take care of yourself at some point," she said simply. "Before it's too late." I went home, quietly undressed, and slipped under the covers next to my partner of eighteen years. I was unable to sleep for a while, mulling over the dinner conversation in my head. I had been here before, and had always just shelved my feelings. This time I couldn't. Over the next few weeks, I became increasingly moody, angry, sad, and sleepless.

On a Friday night, just one month after that unexpectedly pivotal dinner, I ended my relationship of almost two decades. Within a few days, I went downtown in Manhattan to file for my birth certificate and made an appointment for a home study with an agency so that I could adopt a baby from Vietnam.

My gorgeous first son, Ben, adopted from Vietnam when he was an infant, is now ten years old. I adopted a second beautiful son, Des, from Ethiopia when he was six years old and Ben was four. I can't imagine life today without my boys. I also met the love of my life, my partner of eleven years, Diana, and we all live in Maplewood, New Jersey, in a 108-year-old Victorian home, the house of my dreams.

That moment twelve years ago when I listened to a new friend's advice over pasta and salad changed everything for me. I guess I was ready to hear what I hadn't been able to say to myself. And it has made all the difference. Don't shelve your dreams or think that happiness is for other people. Dare to be happy. It's the only way to truly live.

Julie Bowen

Actress, Mother of Three, and Failed Perfectionist

Advice I *Wish* I'd Taken

"Take the C and live forever."

This was the somewhat contradictory advice my seriously type-A father began delivering to me somewhere in my teens. I had vigorously taken up his mantle of overachieving in school and felt that anything less than an A+ was simply subpar. Starting at about age nine, I would lie awake in bed obsessing over the next day's history test, running dates through my mind again and again. (To this day, I can't get rid of good old 1215. Thanks a heap, Magna Carta. Or 1066. Or 1517 . . . The list goes on.) My parents valued education and wanted their daughters to reap the benefits of good schooling, but as they started to see the competitive and self-flagellating monster I was becoming, they adopted a mid-course correction. "Take the C and live forever" became my father's constant refrain. He wanted me to relax and enjoy some of my youth instead of burying any opportunity to have fun under an impossibly high stack of books and an even higher set of expectations.

My parents told me over and over not to put undue pressure on myself—that the big deals of high school would be forgotten in adulthood, but I had my doubts. I tried to have faith in the power of time to erase the jagged edges of tenth-grade embarrassments, yet for years I was haunted by the dastardly split infinitive that took my A+ in Mr. Hollins's English class down to a meager A. That paper on "The Fall of the House of Usher" had become symbolic of just how close perfect was—if only I tried a little harder. . . .

I graduated from high school summa cum laude and magna cum miserable. I was headed off to a prestigious college with a solid academic foundation, but with far too few pleasant memories of high school (making out with Alex Mathews in the darkroom notwithstanding. Thank you, Al). I was, in short, a bit of a grind who continued a library-intense college experience. Yes, I drank myself silly with friends, fell in love for the first time, and discovered the perils of heartbreak, but the overriding theme of my life continued to be "I can do better." I truly believed that if I watched every step carefully I could avoid the pitfalls of a potentially ungraceful entry into the "real world" of work and grown-up responsibilities. In short, I consciously attempted to bypass the normal process of trial and error that everyone else seemed perfectly willing to embrace.

Little did I know.

Three children and a busy work life later, I am astonished at how lucky I am to have all that I have. My kids are healthy, and, when they aren't crying or pooping, they are truly my favorite people. My eternally patient husband puts up with my moods, and, most amazingly, I am paid to hang out and laugh with some incredibly talented people on the set of *Modern Family*. But still, there is a lingering regret. Right now my life is about responsibility and accountability nearly one hundred percent of the time. There isn't one moment of a single day that someone doesn't need something from me. I am, in a word, an adult. An adult with a very fortunate set of responsibilities that my years of perfectionism have equipped me to handle. Yet there are moments when I look back on my years at school and wish that I could make a raft of changes. I would make it messier. I would fail more. I would learn to pick myself up from embarrassment rather than becoming an expert at avoiding it, because "real life," I've discovered, is all about compromise, messiness, and, yes, failure. Real life is learning to lower your expectations while not getting completely blown off course. Real life is about showing your kids that abject failure is not the worst thing that happens, but sometimes the best.

Real life, it turns out—all these years past pop quizzes, exams, and grades—is about taking the C and living forever.

David Axelrod
Political Consultant and Senior Adviser to President Obama

Don't Miss Out on Life

Years ago I was absorbed in establishing my political consulting business. I spent long hours in video editing suites, and many days on the road. I was driven to succeed, oblivious of the toll it was taking on the people I love. My wife, Susan, learned to live as a single parent during campaign seasons. My three young children—Lauren, Michael, and Ethan—became accustomed to missing their dad. And, even when I was home, I was often on the phone, immersed in my work.

Finally, Susan sat me down and gave me advice that was as profound as it was simple. She said, "Don't wake up one day and discover that your kids have grown up and you missed it. It all goes by so quickly."

It was a bracing admonition that I have never forgotten.

As fortunate as I have been in my career, the greatest gift in my life has been Susan and our children. Career can be fickle and success ephemeral. But the love of family is real, reliable, and sustaining.

The kids I carried on my shoulders are all grown now. I can't get back the time we lost. But the most satisfying moments—more than any election night—are still those special occasions when we are together. I now know that these are moments too precious to miss.

Jay Leno
Comedian and Host of *The Tonight Show*

Marry Your Conscience

I've been married for thirty years, and I remember having a discussion with Drew Barrymore on *The Tonight Show,* in which she asked me how you stay married. My advice was: You should always marry your conscience. In Hollywood and just about everywhere else, you're constantly exposed to greed and pride and flattery and lust, and if you meet someone who likewise succumbs to those vices, well, then, you're just screwed. But if you choose to be with someone who says, "What?! You don't usually act like this. Why are you doing *that*?" then you have a pretty good chance of staying on the right path. So I always say marry your conscience. Marry someone who you would want to be, someone who wants to help you be that better version of yourself.

Some people spend more time trying to find the right car than they do trying to find the right mate. They usually base the decision on superficial things. I'm lucky, because I was always very practical in this respect. In my bachelor days if I went out with a woman, no matter how beautiful she was, if I saw her smoking I'd think, Okay, this is going to cost me money down the line—two packs a day and lung cancer, and I'd say right off the bat, "Sorry, babe, this isn't going to work." I remember once, when I was single and in Las Vegas, I saw this incredibly beautiful girl in a casino. I went up to talk to her, and before I knew it we were taking the conversation up to my room. So we're walking toward the elevator, and I asked, "What do you do for a living?" and she answered, "I'm a secretary," and in the next breath she said, "Wait!" She stopped at a roulette wheel and took a hundred bucks out of her purse and shouted "Red!" Well, it went black. "Oh, I lost!" she said lightly. "You just lost one hundred dollars," I said, incredulous, but she just laughed and said, "Oh well!" Right then, I was thinking in my head, I'm outta here. If she can blow her money this quickly, imagine what she'd do with mine! This was in the 1970s, when one hundred dollars was like five hundred dollars today. So I told her this wasn't going to work out and I hightailed it out of there! I think I made the right decision.

I always tell people that I spent the first half of my life trying not to embarrass my mother and the second half trying not to embarrass my wife. It's a good thing to live by. It's always been my mantra: *Oh my God, what if my wife saw this? What if my mom saw this?* It has worked out pretty well.

Jorge Ramos

Emmy Award–Winning Univision News Anchor and Bestselling Author

Find Your Magic

My dad grew up in Mexico City at a time when the only respectable career options for an aspiring college student were in the fields of medicine, engineering, law, and architecture. His own father, my stern and authoritarian grandfather, held unquestioned dominion over his future, and under that pressure my dad "chose" to be an architect. He grew up to become one of those very serious men, the kind who rarely laughed or relaxed. I have but one memory from my childhood of playing soccer with him. One instance. That's it.

But what I do remember more clearly is watching as his melancholic persona somehow morphed—he actually became vibrant and energetic—whenever he was asked to perform a magic trick. There was no excuse small enough to cause the sudden appearance of his special cards or the abrupt flashing of his shining white handkerchief at the table. He would come to life like a muted black-and-white cartoon from the fifties gone totally Pixar. You'd see a twinkle in his eye, a hint of mystery in his expression, and the general sense that here was a man in true connection with his soul.

My three brothers, my sister, and I knew all his tricks by heart. It was really our friends, aunts, and uncles, or any other such unsuspecting visitors, who would prove to be the perfect audience for my father's antics. With their mouths agape and their eyes fixed on my dad's quick hands, these guests would leave our house feeling at once stumped, amused, and impressed. And I don't know what we loved seeing more: my dad's magic tricks themselves or the intoxicating joy that overtook him during a routine. There was no getting around it: Magic made my father's essence shine.

When it came time for me to decide on a career, my father couldn't understand why I chose communications. "What are you going to do with that?" he asked in a way that sounded more like a statement than a question. Of course, he (or his DNA) hoped that I would become a doctor, an engineer, an attorney, or an architect. "I'm not exactly sure, Dad," I responded, "but that's what I really like." Though my path was far from being clear to me (or anyone else) at the time, I wasn't about to let my father take over my life the way my grandfather had taken over his.

Somehow I eventually broke the chain of expectation, became a journalist, moved to the United States (instead of becoming a censored reporter in Mexico), and succeeded as a broadcast anchor and author. I play soccer with my son, Nicolas, almost every week, and I'm proud to say that I outshot my daughter, Paola, the last time we played basketball—a difficult task, given how athletic and smart she is. Whether I'm at work or on the court with one of my kids, I try to remember my dad performing his magic, and in doing so I gently remember to let my own essence shine through.

Ultimately, my father taught me the importance of listening to what makes us truly happy in life. And, at the end of the day, nothing is more magical than that.

Kevin Clash

Co-Executive Producer of "Elmo's World," Director,
Puppet Captain, and Performer of Elmo

What I've Learned from Elmo

The joy I have witnessed when a child meets Elmo for the first time is incredibly overwhelming to me. I often feel like a fly on the wall witnessing pure happiness when Elmo's fans, young and old, greet their furry red *Sesame Street* friend in person.

Nothing is sweeter to me than watching a child, with just a diaper on, coming up to Elmo for a hug. I remember one little girl who actually pulled Elmo off my hand and walked away with him, holding Elmo like a baby. I can still see this child, sitting on her mother's lap, rocking Elmo to sleep. It was such a funny moment.

One day, a young man contacted me about his upcoming tenth wedding anniversary. He wanted Elmo to sign his *Best of Elmo* video as a gift to his wife. He explained that every time he or his wife had a bad day they would come home, put on the *Best of Elmo* video, and it would change their mood instantly.

What I have learned from performing Elmo is that loving and laughter are a gift, and they should be shared every day.

Rosario Dawson

Actress and Activist

———

Feast on Your Life

One of the best pieces of advice that I ever received came recently during a powwow with my dear friend and mentor, Eve Ensler. We've worked together for years, even before I joined the board of V-Day, a global movement she created to end violence against women and children, and our conversations have always been stirring. Eve asked me how I was doing—in that thorough way women have when checking in on each other's journey in life. I told her that I was reevaluating—starting to look at the long term now as a thirty-one-year-old woman and taking stock of my life. I guess Eve sensed that I was feeling a bit anxious because she said, "Rosario, this is your life, your work, your family, your friends. All of these things and people are like heaping plates of food in front of you, and you're getting so caught up in what's next, your food is getting cold. You leave yourself unsatisfied. I say, eat it all up! It will sustain you."

I love food and I remember all of my favorite meals. (I've actually cried eating my mom's pork chops!) How crazy would it be, I thought, if I'd taken only one bite? If I hadn't really committed to the experience in front of me? I realized that what Eve was saying was true. Society tells us to think about *next, next, next* so much so that we never really finish what's in front of us. We taste only a few little bites here and there before ("Ooh, shiny! What's that over there?") moving on to the next plate. We deny our pleasures in order to please. We move too fast: too busy with diets and vigilantly depriving and denying ourselves; fatalistically marrying ourselves to our pain and shame and unhappiness because it's easier. Why? Why won't we let ourselves be happy? Why do we feel that everyone else but us deserves bliss? Even when things are going well, we're so apprehensive that the other shoe *might* drop that we miss the moment.

Instead, as Eve told me, we need to learn to sit down and eat that meal that is our life. Really consume it. And I'm not talking about stuffing yourself with "stuff" to fill the void but consuming real nourishment. Enjoy every step of the journey, not just the choice bits and the peaks that society deems important. All of it is important—so let it in! Fill up on every experience life has in store. It's your life, and it's right in front of you. You can't save it for later, so get down to cleaning your plate and licking your fingers. Taste what life has to offer. Savor it. Enjoy the feast!

Russell Baker

Pulitzer Prize–Winning Author and Columnist

Ten Ways to Avoid Mucking Up the World Any Worse Than It Already Is

One: Bend down once in a while and smell a flower.

Two: Don't go around in clothes that talk. There is already too much talk in the world. We've got so many talking people there's hardly anybody left to listen. With radio and television and telephones, we've got talking furniture. With bumper stickers, we've got talking cars. Talking clothes just add to the uproar. If you simply cannot resist being an incompetent klutz, don't boast about it by wearing a T-shirt that says UNDERACHIEVER AND PROUD OF IT. Being dumb is not the worst thing in the world, but letting your clothes shout it out loud depresses the neighbors and embarrasses your parents.

Point three follows from point two, and it's this: Listen once in a while. It's amazing what you can hear. On a hot summer day in the country, you can hear the corn growing, the crack of a tin roof buckling under the power of the sun. In a real, old-fashioned parlor silence so deep that you can hear the dust settling on the velveteen settee, you might hear the footsteps of something sinister gaining on you, or a heart-stoppingly beautiful strain from Mozart that you haven't heard since childhood, or the voice of somebody—now gone—whom you loved. Or sometime when you're talking up a storm so brilliant, so charming that you can hardly believe how wonderful you are, pause for just a moment and listen to yourself. It's good for the soul to hear yourself as others hear you, and next time maybe, just maybe, you won't talk so much, so loudly, so brilliantly, so charmingly, so utterly shamefully foolishly.

Four: Sleep in the nude. In an age when people don't even get dressed to go to the theater anymore, it's silly getting dressed up to go to bed. What's more, now that you can no longer smoke, drink gin, or eat bacon and eggs without somebody trying to make you feel ashamed of yourself, sleeping in the nude is one deliciously sinful pleasure that you can commit without being caught by the Puritan police squads that patrol the nation.

Five: Turn off the TV once or twice a month and pick up a book. It will ease your blood pressure. It might even wake up your mind, but if it puts you to sleep you're still a winner. Better to sleep than have to watch that endless parade of body bags the local news channel marches through your parlor.

Six: Don't take your gun to town. Don't even leave it at home unless you lock all your bullets in a safe-deposit box in a faraway bank. The surest way to get shot is not to drop by the nearest convenience store for a bottle of milk at midnight but to keep a loaded pistol in your own house. What about your constitutional right to bear arms, you say. I would simply point out that you don't have to exercise a constitutional right just because you have it. You have the constitutional right to run for president of the United States, but most people have too much sense to insist on exercising it.

Seven: Learn to fear the automobile. It is not the trillion-dollar deficit that will finally destroy America. It is the automobile. Congressional studies of future highway needs are terrifying. A typical projection shows that when your generation is middle-aged, Interstate 95 between Miami and Fort Lauderdale will have to be twenty-two lanes wide to avert total paralysis of South Florida. Imagine an entire country covered with asphalt. My grandfather's generation shot horses. Yours had better learn to shoot automobiles.

Eight: Have some children. Children add texture to your life. They will save you from turning into old fogies before you're middle-aged. They will teach you humility. When old age overtakes you—as it inevitably will, I'm sorry to say—having a few children will provide you with people who will feel guilty when they're accused of being ungrateful for all you've done for them. It's almost impossible nowadays to find anybody who will feel guilty about anything, including mass murder. When you reach the golden years, your best bet is children, the ingrates.

Nine: Get married. I know you don't want to hear this, but getting married will give you a lot more satisfaction in the long run than your BMW. It provides a standard set of parents for your children and gives you that second income you will need when it's time to send those children to college. What's more, without marriage you'll have practically no material at all to work with when you decide to write a book or hire a psychiatrist.

When you get married, whatever you do, do not ask a lawyer to draw up a marriage contract spelling out how your lives will be divvied up when you get divorced. It's hard enough making a marriage work without having a blueprint for its destruction drawn up before you go to the altar. Speaking of lawyers brings me to point nine and a half, which is: Avoid lawyers unless you have nothing to do with the rest of your life but kill time.

And, finally, point ten: smile. You're one of the luckiest people in the world. You're living in America. Enjoy it. When you're out in the world, you're going to find yourself surrounded by shouting, red-in-the-face, stomping-mad politicians, radio yakmeisters and, yes, sad to say, newspaper columnists, telling you "you never had it so bad" and otherwise trying to spoil your day. When they come at you with that, ladies and gentlemen, give them a wink and a smile and a good view of your departing back. And, as you stroll away, bend down and smell a flower.

Wendy Walker
Senior Executive Producer of *Larry King Live*,
Senior Vice-President of CNN, and Author of *Producer*

Positive Energy Is the New Pink

The older I get, the more convinced I am that there is something to positive and negative energy. I'm really living by this now. Some take it to a more intense level, such as not eating meat from unhappy animals who have lived uncivilized lives. They say that the unhappy energy goes into our bodies and causes us to be unhappy, too. There may be something to that, but I haven't taken it that far yet. I'm simply trusting my intuition more these days, as I try to keep in the company of positive people and thus positive energy. I still like hamburgers.

When I wake up every morning, before I get out of bed, I remind myself of what I'm grateful for. It starts my day off right and makes me feel good about what's in front of me. I think about my children and our health and all the love I have in my life. However hard we try to surround ourselves with people who are good and who care about us, though, there will always be those who, for some reason, have negative energy. They can be hurtful and cause you sadness or pain.

My grandmother used to say, "Kill them with kindness." Another strategy is: "Keep your friends close and your enemies closer." There is a lot of wisdom in these two old sayings. Instead of trying to get revenge, take the high road. Let it go. Instead of trying to get back at someone because she has hurt you, think of one nice thing about that person and put that out into the universe instead. If you don't let it go, that person's negativity will stay inside you, and that's exactly where you don't want that energy to be.

So the next time you're hurt by someone, wish that person well in your heart and tell your brain to move on and think about something else that really matters. You will be amazed at how it releases your negative energy. People can't control you if you won't let them.

And, as much as you can, surround yourself with people who love you and want you to be happy. Do it. I simply will not compromise anymore with my heart. I avoid people who are not genuine and whose energy is toxic. Instead of internalizing the negative emotions of these people, forgive them for being unhappy souls. That goes for a friend, a co-worker, a lover, or even the guy who stole the parking space you were waiting so patiently for. Any frustration you can guard your body from, do it. Forgive, let go, breathe, and respond to these negative energies with love. You will be amazed at how much lighter, happier, and healthier you feel.

Eric Stonestreet

Emmy Award–Winning Actor

---

but mostly, have a really fun time

follow your fear
prepare don't plan
do what you say
say what you mean
know what you don't know
don't hold yourself to other people's standards
own a pet
call your parents
create a comfortable living space
be happy for other people
cultivate friendships
stand up for those who can't stand up for themselves
understand what realistic expectations are
don't lie
get to know your gut and then listen to it
say you're sorry before you're too embarrassed to
always wear clean underwear
be on time
be nice to receptionists
appreciate other people's talents
identify people who don't have your best interests in mind
people will disappoint you
people will amaze you
people will inspire you
overlisten

you will disappoint people

you will amaze people

you will inspire people

don't drink too much alcohol

remember that the old lady who's taking forever in line is someone's
    grandma

be curious

ask questions

give yourself a break

have truthful conversations with yourself

think about your day in the shower

reflect on your day before you fall asleep

reward yourself from time to time

have a good clean joke at the ready

have a good dirty joke at the ready

silence can be golden

have someone you admire evaluate your handshake

be humbly confident

smell good

don't let the highs be too high, so the lows aren't too low

get to know you

learn to like you

let people love you

no one does you better than you

want what you have and you'll have what you want

lead with justice and judge with mercy

don't let your mouth overload your rear

DOING THE BEST WE CAN

As we have seen in these pages, the best advice—the stick-to-your-ribs kind—comes from many sources, sometimes from those in our own homes, but often from people unknown to our small circles. In 2008, *The Wall Street Journal* published an essay written in 1938 by a man named Ned Carpenter called "Before I Die." It outlined what one young American boy from Wilmington, Delaware, dreamed of doing and being. It detailed a series of surprising goals he set for himself. Carpenter was a hero in World War II and became a highly revered lawyer. After he died, days before Christmas three years ago, his wife, Carroll, pulled the essay from a drawer, where she had kept it for decades. She would read it on occasion, for inspiration. What is most stunning, and important to note, is that Carpenter was just seventeen years old when he wrote it. I didn't know Mr. Carpenter, but I believe he was on to something. I leave you with his words.

Edmund N. Carpenter II

War Hero, Lawyer and Criminal Justice Advocate,
Father (1921–2008)

―――

Before I Die

It may seem very strange to the reader that one of my tender age should already be thinking about that inevitable end to which even the paths of glory lead. However, this essay is not really concerned with death, but rather with life, my future life. I have set down here the things which I, at this age, believe essential to happiness and complete enjoyment of life. Some of them will doubtless seem very odd to the reader; others will perhaps be completely in accord with his own wishes. At any rate, they compose a synopsis of the things which I sincerely desire to have done before I leave this world and pass on to the life hereafter or to oblivion.

Before I die I want to know that I have done something truly great, that I have accomplished some glorious achievement the credit for which belongs solely to me. I do not aspire to become as famous as a Napoleon and conquer many nations; but I do want, almost above all else, to feel that I have been an addition to this world of ours. I should like the world, or at least my native land, to be proud of me and to sit up and take notice when my name is pronounced and say, "There is a man who has done a great thing." I do not want to have passed through life as just another speck of humanity, just another cog in a tremendous machine. I want to be something greater, far greater, than that. My desire is not so much for immortality as for distinction while I am alive. When I leave this world, I want to know that my life has not been in vain, but that I have, in the course of my existence, done something of which I am rightfully very proud.

Before I die I want to know that during my life I have brought great happiness to others. Friendship, we all agree, is one of the best things in the world, and I want to have many friends. But I could never die fully contented unless I knew that those with whom I had been intimate had gained real happiness from their friendship with me. Moreover, I feel there is a really sincere pleasure to be found in pleasing others, a kind of pleasure that can not be gained from anything else. We all want much happiness in our lives, and giving it to others is one of the surest ways to achieve it for ourselves.

Before I die I want to have visited a large portion of the globe and to have actually lived with several foreign races in their own environment. By traveling in countries other than my own I hope to broaden and improve my outlook on life so that I can get a deeper and more complete satisfaction from living. By mixing the weighty philosophy of China with the hard practicalism of America, I hope to make my life fuller. By blending the rigid discipline of Germany with the great liberty in our own nation I hope to more completely enjoy my years on this earth. These are but two examples of the many things which I expect to achieve by traveling and thus have a greater appreciation of life.

Before I die, there is another great desire I must fulfill, and that is to have felt a truly great love. At my young age I know that love, other than some filial affection, is probably far beyond my ken. Yet, young as I may be, I believe I have had enough inkling of the subject to know that he who has not loved has not really lived. Nor will I feel my life is complete until I have actually experienced that burning flame and know that I am at last in love, truly in love. I want to feel that my whole heart and soul are set on one girl whom I wish to be a perfect angel in my eyes. I want to feel a love that will far surpass any other emotion that I have ever felt. I know that when I am at last really in love then I will start living a different, better life, filled with new pleasures that I never knew existed.

Before I die I want to feel a great sorrow. This, perhaps, of all my wishes will seem the strangest to the reader. Yet, is it unusual that I should wish to have had a complete life? I want to have lived fully, and certainly sorrow is a part of life. It is my belief that, as in the case of love, no man has lived until he has felt sorrow. It molds us and teaches us that there is a far deeper significance to life than might be supposed if one passed through this world forever happy and carefree. Moreover, once the pangs of sorrow have slackened, for I do not believe it to be a permanent emotion, its dregs often leave us a better knowledge of this world of ours and a better understanding of humanity. Yes, strange as it may seem, I really want to feel a great sorrow.

With this last wish I complete the synopsis of the things I want to do before I die. Irrational as they may seem to the reader, nevertheless they comprise a sincere summary of what I truthfully now believe to be the things most essential to a fully satisfactory and happy life. As I stand here on the threshold of my future, these are the things which to me seem the most valuable. Perhaps in fifty years I will think that they are extremely silly. Perhaps I will wonder, for instance, why I did not include a wish for continued happiness. Yet, right now, I do not desire my life to be a bed of roses. I want it to be something much more than that. I want it to be a truly great adventure, never dull, always exciting and engrossing; not sickly sweet, yet not unhappy. And I believe it will be all I wish if I do these things before I die.

As for death itself, I do not believe that it will be such a disagreeable thing provided my life has been successful. I have always considered life and death as two cups of wine. Of the first cup, containing the wine of life, we can learn a little from literature and from those who have drunk it, but only a little. In order to get the full flavor we must drink deeply of it for ourselves. I believe that after I have quaffed the cup containing the wine of life, emptied it to its last dregs, then I will not fear to turn to that other cup, the one whose contents can be designated only by X, an unknown, and a thing about which we can gain no knowledge at all until we drink for ourselves. Will it be sweet, or sour, or tasteless? Who can tell? Surely none of us like to think of death as the end of everything. Yet is it? That is a question that for all of us will one day be answered when we, having witnessed the drama of life, come to the final curtain. Probably we will all regret to leave this world, yet I believe that after I have drained the first cup, and have possibly grown a bit weary of its flavor, I will then turn not unwillingly to the second cup and to the new and thrilling experience of exploring the unknown.

ACKNOWLEDGMENTS

There would be no book without this amazing group of people who took the time out of their ridiculously busy lives to write about dreams dashed, goals reached, courage mustered, and lives changed. To all of you, thank you for being a part of this effort. It means the world to me. I brought this idea to my wonderful friend Susan Mercandetti, executive editor of Random House, with my typical preface of "This may sound crazy, but . . ." Thank you, Susan, for thinking this wasn't crazy and for your patience and guidance as I navigated the unfamiliar world of publishing. Robin Rolewicz Duchnowski (I know, a mouthful!) is the real hero behind this book. She rolled up her sleeves and got the job done, professionally, coolly, and enthusiastically, even while nursing her ten-month-old daughter Polly's bad case of chicken pox. Robin, you are a rock star. And Ben Steinberg's invaluable help and hipster persona kept things on track and on time. (Well, mostly, right, Ben?)

And from Scholarship America, Janine Fugate, Lauren A. Segal, and Terrence Kraling: We are united in our goal of having more kids go to, as well as graduate from, college.

I have been graced with a strong, devoted family and friends who have stuck by me throughout the many passages in my life. You have been there every step of the way and I love and treasure you all. As we learn in this book, everyone needs a cheerleader, and I want to mention some other members of my squad who have always cheered me on. Jeff Zucker, Andy Lack, Rick Kaplan—what would I do without you guys? And Matthew Hiltzik and Kevin Goldman—thank you for your wise counsel and wicked senses of humor. To Lori Beecher, Lauren Osborn, and Brittany Jones-Cooper—my go-to girls and partners in crime— thank you . . . for everything. Through the dark days and the sunny ones, I am left with one irrefutable thought: I've been blessed. And for that I am grateful.

SOURCE NOTES/PERMISSIONS ACKNOWLEDGMENTS

Some comments by the author, Katie Couric, have been adapted from speeches and commencement addresses delivered at institutions such as Case Western Reserve University, Princeton University, and Williams College.

Al Abdullah, Rania, "Through Other Eyes." © Her Majesty Queen Rania Al Abdullah. Used by permission.

Albom, Mitch, "Giving Is Living." © 2011 by Mitch Albom, Inc. Used by permission.

Albright, Madeleine K., "Never Play Hide-and-Seek with the Truth." © Madeleine K. Albright. Used by permission.

Amanpour, Christiane, "Thank You, Colonel Shaki." © Christiane Amanpour. Used by permission.

Angelou, Maya, "Make Your Own Path." © Dr. Maya Angelou. Used by permission.

Applegate, Christina, "You Don't Have the Luxury of Negative Thought." © Christina Applegate. Used by permission.

Aronson, Jane, M.D., "Dare to Be Happy." © Dr. Jane Aronson. Used by permission.

Axelrod, David, "Don't Miss Out on Life." © David Axelrod. Used by permission.

Baker, Russell, "Ten Ways to Avoid Mucking Up the World Any Worse Than It Already Is." Adapted from *Not Mucking Up the World Any Worse Than It Already Is,* Copyright © 1995 by Russell Baker. Used by permission of Don Congdon Associates, Inc.

Banks, Tyra, "SMIZE . . . with Your Booty." © 2010 by Bankable Books, LLC. Used by permission.

Batali, Mario, "Life Is Not a Recipe." Adapted from a commencement address at Rutgers University, with permission of the author. © Mario Batali. Used by permission.

Beyoncé, "Take Time to Know Yourself." © Beyoncé Knowles. Used by permission.

Bloomberg, Michael, "The Real Eighty Percent." © Michael R. Bloomberg. Used by permission.

Bowen, Julie, "Advice I *Wish* I'd Taken." © Julie Bowen. Used by permission.

Brees, Drew, "Use Adversity as an Opportunity." © Drew Brees. Used by permission.

Burns, Ken, "Do Something Lasting." Adapted from a commencement address at Lehigh University, with permission of the author. © 2008 by Ken Burns. All rights reserved. Used by permission.

Calhoun, David L., "Develop Your Own Brand of Self-Confidence." Adapted from a commencement address at Virginia Polytechnic Institute and State University, with permission of the author. © David L. Calhoun. Used by permission.

Carpenter, Edmund N., II, "Before I Die." © 1938 by Edmund Carpenter. Used by permission of the Estate of Edmund Carpenter.

Carter, Jimmy, "Always Do Your Best." © President Jimmy Carter. Used by permission.

Case, Scott, "You're Sitting on a Winning Lottery Ticket—Invest It Wisely." Adapted from a commencement address at Greenwich High School, with permission of the author. © T. Scott Case. Used by permission.

Chenault, Ken, "Face History and Make History." Adapted from a commencement address at Howard University, with permission of the author. © Kenneth I. Chenault. Used by permission.

Clash, Kevin, "What I've Learned from Elmo." © Clash Puppets, Inc. Used by permission.

Clinton, William J., "Be a Good Citizen." © William J. Clinton. Used by permission.

Colbert, Stephen, "Yes . . . and That's the Word." © Stephen Colbert. Used by permission.

Collins, Gail, "Ask, and Ye Shall Receive." © Gail Collins. Used by permission.

Cosby, Bill, "Don't Be Your Own Worst Enemy." Adapted, with permission from the author, from "The Day I Decided to Quit Show Business, or The Night I Met the Enemy and It Was I," in *Cosbyology: Essays and Observations from the Doctor of Comedy* (New York: Hyperion, 2001). © 2001 William H. Cosby, Jr. Used by permission.

Crow, Sheryl, "Do the Best You Can." © Sheryl Crow. Used by permission.

David, Larry, "Curb Your Enthusiasm, Please." © Larry David. Used by permission.

Dawson, Rosario, "Feast on Your Life." © Rosario Dawson. Used by permission.

DeGeneres, Ellen, "Be True to Yourself." Adapted from a commencement address at Tulane University, with permission of the author. © Ellen DeGeneres. Used by permission.

Doyne, Maggie, "Everything You Need Is Everything You Have." © Maggie Doyne. Used by permission.

Evert, Chris, "Get Off the Sidelines!" © Chris Evert. Used by permission.

Ferguson, Craig, "Hurry Up and Take Your Time." © Craig Ferguson. Used by permission.

Fox, Michael J., "Be Grateful." © 2011 Michael J. Fox. Used by permission.

Freeman, Morgan, "You Quit, You Fail." © Morgan Freeman. Used by permission.

Friedman, Thomas, "Be a Skeptic, Not a Cynic" and "Be an Untouchable, Do What You Love." Adapted from a commencement address at Williams College, with permission of the author. © Thomas Friedman. Used by permission.

Garten, Ina, "If You Love Doing It, You'll Be Very Good at It." © Ina Garten. Used by permission.

Gates, Melinda, "The Sky's the Limit." © 2011 Bill & Melinda Gates Foundation. Used by permission.

Gladwell, Malcolm, "Don't Turn on Your Greatest Asset." © Malcolm Gladwell. Used by permission.

Goldberg, Whoopi, "Do Unto Others." © Whoopi Goldberg. Used by permission.

Goldman, Matt, "I Don't Want to Be Reasonable." Adapted from a commencement address at the Ross School, with permission of the author. © Matt Goldman. Used by permission.

Guggenheim, Davis, "Don't Listen to Can't." © Davis Guggenheim. Used by permission.

Handler, Chelsea, "Pay Attention!" © Chelsea Handler. Used by permission.

Hsieh, Tony, "Be Lucky." © Tony Hsieh. Used by permission.

Huffington, Arianna, "A Lot of Greek Chutzpah." © Arianna Huffington. Used by permission.

Immelt, Jeff, "Be Humbled by What You Don't Know." Adapted from a commencement address at Boston College, with permission of the author. © Jeffrey Immelt. Used by permission.

Jackman, Hugh, "Trust Your Gut." © Hugh Jackman. Used by permission.

Jonas, Kevin, Joe, and Nick, "Remember Where You Come From." © 2011 Jonas Brothers Enterprises, LLC. Used by permission.

Kent, Muhtar, "In Good Times and in Bad." © Muhtar Kent. Used by permission.

Keys, Alicia, "The Question." © Alicia Keys. Used by permission.

Kimmel, Jimmy, "Wisdom You Can Eat." © 2010 Jimmy Kimmel. Used by permission.

King, Larry, "Learn How to Listen." © Larry King. Used by permission.

Kwan, Michelle, "Fall Down and Get Back Up." © Michelle Kwan. Used by permission.

Lauer, Matt, "Sometimes You Gotta Go Off Course." © Matt Lauer. Used by permission.

Leno, Jay, "Be Open to Other People," "In Defense of Class Clowns," and "Marry Your Conscience." © Jay Leno. Used by permission.

Levine, Ellen, "Get Over Yourself." © Ellen Levine. Used by permission.

Ling, Lisa, "Give of Yourself." © Lisa Ling. Used by permission.

Linney, Laura, "Never Read Your Own Reviews." Adapted from a commencement address at the Juilliard School, with permission of the author. © Laura Linney. Used by permission.

Lopez, George, "Fortune Favors the Bold." © George Lopez. Used by permission.

Lynch, Jane, "Life Is a Series of Happy Accidents." © Jane Lynch. Used by permission.

Marsalis, Wynton, "Commit with Your Whole Heart." © Wynton Marsalis. Used by permission.

Martin, Steve, "Take Chances." © Steve Martin. Used by permission.

Mayer, Marissa, "When There Isn't a Right Choice . . ." © Marissa A. Mayer. Used by permission.

McConaughey, Matthew, "You Were Just Having Trouble." © Matthew McConaughey. Used by permission.

McGraw, "Dr. Phil," "Get Excited About Your Life." © Dr. Phil McGraw. Used by permission.

Mirren, Helen, "Beware of Fear." © Helen Mirren. Used by permission.

Molina, Raúl de, "Against Apparent Odds, Never Give Up." © Raúl de Molina. Used by permission.

Mo'Nique, "Not Going Through It . . . Growing Through It." © Mo'Nique. Used by permission.

Moore, Wes, "Have Faith, Not Fear." © Wes Moore. Used by permission.

Nooyi, Indra, "Opportunity Will Find You." Adapted from a commencement address at the Pennsylvania State University, with permission of the author. © Indra K. Nooyi. Used by permission.

Novogratz, Jacqueline, "Commit to Something Bigger Than Yourself." © Jacqueline Novogratz. Used by permission.

Oates, Joyce Carol, "'Here Is Life . . .'" © Ontario Review, Inc. Used by permission.

O'Brien, Soledad, "Push Beyond Prejudice." © Soledad O'Brien. Used by permission.

Odierno, General Ray (U.S. Army), "Real Success." © General Ray Odierno. Used by permission.

Ohno, Apolo, "It's Not About the Forty Seconds." © Apolo Ohno. Used by permission.

Orman, Suze, "Do What Is Right, Not What Is Easy." © Suze Orman. Used by permission.

Oz, Mehmet, M.D., "Take Time to Really Listen." © Dr. Mehmet Oz. Used by permission.

Petraeus, General David H., "Be Comfortable with the Uncomfortable." © General David H. Petraeus. Used by permission.

Plame, Valerie, "Life Is Unfair." © Valerie Plame Wilson. Used by permission.

Powell, Colin, "It Doesn't Matter Where You Start." © Colin Powell. Used by permission.

Quindlen, Anna, "Courage Is the Ultimate Career Move." © Anna Quindlen. Used by permission.

Ramos, Jorge, "Find Your Magic." © Jorge Ramos, Univision News. Used by permission.

Rice, Condoleezza, "Find Your Next Adventure." © Dr. Condoleezza Rice. Used by permission.

Roberts, Robin, "Determination Makes the Difference." © Robin Roberts. Used by permission.

Rodriguez, Alex, "The Power of Words." © Alex Rodriguez. Used by permission.

Roker, Al, "Willard's Way." © Al Roker. Used by permission.

Rushdie, Salman, "Angela's Asterisks." © Salman Rushdie. Used by permission.

Salinas, Maria Elena, "You Never Stop Learning." © Maria E. Salinas. Used by permission.

Schieffer, Bob, "Momo's Rules." © Bob Schieffer. Used by permission.

Schmidt, Eric, "Say Yes." © Eric Schmidt. Used by permission.

Seacrest, Ryan, "The Hardest-Working Guy in Showbiz." © Ryan Seacrest. Used by permission.

Shaiman, Marc, *"Oh, Miss Midler . . ."* © Marc Shaiman. Used by permission.

Shriver, Maria, "Don't Be Afraid of Being Afraid." Adapted, with permission of the author, from *One More Thing Before You Go* (New York: Free Press, 2005). © Maria Shriver. Used by permission.

Shyamalan, M. Night, "Sadness." © M. Night Shyamalan. Used by permission.

Simmons, Ruth J., "A Cold Bucket of Water." © Ruth J. Simmons. Used by permission.

Sirleaf, Ellen Johnson, "No Job Is Small." Adapted, with permission of the author, from *This Child Will Be Great: Memoir of a Remarkable Life by Africa's First Woman President* (New York: HarperCollins, 2009). © Ellen Johnson Sirleaf. Used by permission.

Sittenfeld, Curtis, "My Other (Less Neurotic) Half." © Curtis Sittenfeld. Used by permission.

Smiley, Tavis, "Fail Better." © Tavis Smiley. Used by permission.

Spielberg, Steven, "Listen and Learn." © Steven Spielberg. Used by permission.

Stanton, Phil, "Inspiration Lives in Unexpected Places." Adapted from a commencement address at the Ross School, with permission of the author. © Phil Stanton. Used by permission.

ABOUT THE AUTHOR

KATIE COURIC is the anchor and managing editor of the *CBS Evening News with Katie Couric,* a *60 Minutes* correspondent, and anchor of CBS News prime-time specials. She has covered most of the major breaking news events over the past fifteen years, including the historic presidential election of 2008, the September 11 attacks, the Columbine tragedy, the Oklahoma City bombing, and the funeral of Princess Diana.